The Collection's at the Core

The Collection's at the Core

Revitalize Your Library with Innovative Resources for the Common Core and STEM

Marcia A. Mardis

 **LIBRARIES UNLIMITED**

AN IMPRINT OF ABC-CLIO, LLC
Santa Barbara, California • Denver, Colorado • Oxford, England

Library of Congress Cataloging-in-Publication Data

Mardis, Marcia A.
  The collection's at the core : revitalize your library with innovative resources for the Common Core and STEM / Marcia A. Mardis.
      pages   cm
  Includes bibliographical references and index.
  ISBN 978-1-61069-504-6 (paperback) — ISBN 978-1-61069-505-3 (ebook)
1. School libraries—Collection development—United States.   2. Libraries—Special collections—Electronic information resources.   3. Libraries—Special collections—Science. 4. Libraries—Special collections—Technology.   5. Libraries—Special collections—Engineering. 6. Libraries—Special collections—Mathematics.   7. Science—Study and teaching—Digital libraries—United States.   8. Science—Study and teaching—United States—Computer network resources.   9. School librarian participation in curriculum planning—United States.   10. Open access publishing.   I. Title.
  Z675.S3M265   2015
  025.2'1878—dc23   2014027766

ISBN: 978-1-61069-504-6
EISBN: 978-1-61069-505-3

19 18 17 16 15   1 2 3 4 5

This book is also available on the World Wide Web as an eBook.
Visit www.abc-clio.com for details.

Libraries Unlimited
An Imprint of ABC-CLIO, LLC

ABC-CLIO, LLC
130 Cremona Drive, P.O. Box 1911
Santa Barbara, California 93116-1911

This book is printed on acid-free paper ∞
Manufactured in the United States of America

Excerpts reprinted with permission from *A Framework for K-12 Science Education: Practices, Crosscutting Concepts, and Core Ideas* (2012) and the National Science Education Standards (1996) by the National Academy of Sciences, Courtesy of the National Academies Press, Washington, D.C.

Contents

Preface

STEM for Our Students: Content to Co-Conspiracy?

Kaye Howe
Founding Director, National Science Digital Library

It all seemed relatively straightforward. In the world where many of us grew up, content was scarce and access often was difficult—sometimes even exotic. Who did not dream of a summer at the Folger Shakespeare Library or the Bibliotheque Nationale, poring over manuscripts, for which part of the allure was that they were hard to find and even harder to access? For those of us who became librarians in an age when print dominated, we find ourselves confronting new ideas about what we should collect, how we should ensure access, and who we can be in our schools.

When the National Science Digital Library (NSDL) started—now a decade ago—vastly expanded access to digital content seemed, almost in and of itself, transformational. One of the foundational and iconic documents of NSDL, *Pathways to Progress: Vision and Plans for Developing the NSDL*, written in March of 2001, opened with this statement:

> The National Science, Mathematics, Engineering, and Technology Education Digital Library was conceived and is being constructed to support excellence in SMET (now STEM) education for all Americans. The NSDL will be a comprehensive information system built as a distributed network and will develop and make accessible collections of high-quality resources for instruction at all levels and in all educational settings. (Manduca, McMartin, and Mogk 2001, 2–3)

Even at that early moment, our colleagues realized that more than good content was needed, that the digital world gave us access to another valuable resource—connection. The authors went on to say the following about digital learning resources:

> They will also establish and maintain communications networks to facilitate interactions and collaborations among all (STEM) educators and learners, and will foster

development of new communities of learners in (STEM) education. (Manduca, McMartin, and Mogk 2001, 6)

This was—and is—a compelling vision. Education, in so many ways, is the nation's common ground, and the Internet gave us the means to expand and enhance the community of educators and learners, to share scientific knowledge, to link the world of research to the world of the classroom, and to increase the speed of knowledge dissemination. Vast collections of STEM digital resources—some of which are featured in this volume— have embraced this idea of cultivating community with cut- ting-edge tools and services that allow educators to connect with one another to bring STEM teaching and learning to active, vibrant life. Day and night, the digital libraries hum with dis- cussions, recommendations, and support for literature lovers, weekend biologists, and educators striving to create excellent STEM education experiences for all learners.

The researchers from Project Tomorrow (http://tomorrow.org) bring us that evolving reality every year with their *Speak Up!* sur- vey results. Since they began in 2003, well over a million and a half students, teachers, administrators, parents and, recently, pre-service teachers, respond to their survey about the use of technology in the classroom. They release the results every year in Washington, D.C., and in 2010, Project Tomorrow CEO Julie Evans laid out the #1 trend they saw in 2009 *Speak Up* data—the Free Agent Learner (Project Tomorrow 2010). Here's the profile of that learner:

- Self-directed
- Untethered to traditional education
- Expert at personal data aggregation
- Knows the power of connections
- Creates new communities
- Not tethered to physical networks
- Values experiential learning—make it real and relevant
- Content developer
- Process as important as knowledge

In many, many ways, that Free Agent Learner is every teacher's dream. Nevertheless, that Learner is challenging, and disrup- tive of the order and authority of the classroom that has been comfortable to us, however much we ourselves might have complained about its limitations. That Learner, and more of them, we assume, every year, must find the traditional classroom more constraining, even less relevant, every year.

Not that we, as librarians, don't articulate an understanding of disjunction ourselves. Dave Yaron, a longtime NSDL community member and professor of chemistry at Carnegie Mellon wrote (Yaron 2009):

> Many of these challenges (facing libraries' support for digital learning) arise from juxtaposing the formal education system, which is shockingly resistant to change, with the Internet, which is shockingly able to undergo radical transformations on a moment's notice. Life at the interface of these differently paced worlds can instill a professional version of manic depression. Ideas intended to radically improve education most often end up having incremental impacts.

We must not be content with the incremental impacts; (t)o move beyond (them) we must understand the user. Digital resources have all sorts of users, but, arguably, the most significant for educational impact, look very like that of Project Tomorrow's "Free Agent Learner." To help us, see Mizuko Itō et al. and their book, *Hanging Out, Messing Around, and Geeking Out: Kids Living and Learning with New Media*, part of the John D. and Catherine T. MacArthur Foundation Series in Digital Media and Learning (Itō 2010).

Until you have a chance to read it yourself, here are some of its illuminating observations, based on watching kids and their communities:

> Educators and policy makers need to understand that participation in the digital age means more than being able to access "serious" online information and culture; it also means the ability to participate in social and recreational activities online. This requires a cultural shift and a certain openness to experimentation and social exploration that generally is not characteristic of educational institutions. . . . On the interest-driven side of the equation, the ways in which we have sheltered youth from workplaces and institutionalized them in age-segregated schools means that there are few opportunities for youth to see adults as peers. . . . When kids have the opportunity to gain access to accomplished elders in areas where they

are interested in developing expertise, an accessible and immediate aspirational trajectory . . . can be created. (Itō 2010, 347, 350)

And, as they move from vision to dream:

> Kids' participation in networked publics suggests new ways to think about the role of public education. Rather than thinking of public education as a burden that schools must shoulder on their own, what would it mean to think of public education as a responsibility of a more distributed network of people and institutions? And rather than assuming that education is primarily about preparing kids for jobs and careers, what would it mean to think of education as a process of guiding kids' participation in public life more generally, a public life that includes social, recreational, and civic engagement? And finally, what would it mean to enlist help in this endeavor from an engaged and diverse set of publics that are broader than what we think of as educational and civic institutions? (Itō 2010, 352–53)

We all understand the investment we have in formal education and its institutions, and we all honor those who, day after day, labor there. Given the ubiquity, agility, and flexibility of the Internet, given the deep commitment of communities like the NSDL's developers and users, and given the desire we all share to understand the whole range of education, we should take these observations to heart and apply them, as best we can, in our well-known contexts including the school library.

We have, as librarians who build and promote dynamic library collections, a powerful resource for educational impact, if we can genuinely interact with that youthful user. Can we become, as *Hanging Out* describes (Itō 2010, 349), "co-conspirators" in their education? And, can we use resources like the NSDL to ensure that we reach all of our students in the school library? How can we be vehicles for inclusion as well as expansion?

We have much demanding work to do in school libraries to support STEM learning. NSDL—with its content, through its technologies, and using its network of trusted partners, we can further understanding of the vexed and demanding role of STEM in student learning. School librarians can be vital links between digital resources and school-based users.

More than a decade later, for librarians as well as for STEM teachers and learners, it is clear that we are in a genuinely new place and we need to understand and participate in that geography. Remember Joel 2:28, *"your old men shall dream dreams, your young men shall see visions"* (King James Cambridge Version 1995).

Co-conspirators all!

Adapted from M. A. Mardis and K. Howe,
"STEM for Our Students: Content or Co-Conspiracy?"
Knowledge Quest, 39 (2), 8–11 (2010)

A Note from the Author

I often say that what I don't know could fill a book. It would appear that what I *do* know could fill a book, too! I present you with a culmination of experiences—a story I have had the privilege to live and now to tell you.

As a school librarian who began earnest practice in a private Texas school for science and mathematics, I saw the central role that the school library could have in students' learning in these two areas. Whether it was helping students connect with experts via phone and email; teaching students to make better tables and charts for their science fair projects; fine-tuning the collection to not just support science and mathematics and their applications to fine arts and literature studies; or helping students lose themselves in science fiction, fantasy, and graphic novels, the dynamic and leading librarian I had read about in my MLS coursework became my professional self. Thomas Dolby might have been blinded by science, but my career was made by it.

In 1998, my journey took a bit of a turn. On the tail of the disruptive National Science Foundation–sponsored NSFNET project that brought the Internet to universities, colleges, public libraries, and schools, I joined the organization tasked with promoting the many uses of this new Internet technology in teaching and learning. Educators could not see what they did not know, and I was one of the people that helped them to see the possibilities. In 1999, the National Science Foundation began providing funding for me and my treasured colleagues to build a National Science Digital Library (NSDL), which would organize, describe, make available, and promote digital resources that would support science, technology, engineering, and mathematics (STEM) learning. This turn was the perfect direction because in it I found the perfect blend of school and digital librarianship.

The NSDL has given me a seat at the table for some of the most important education policy developments of the last 15 years. The story I tell here is borne of the growing ubiquity of the Internet, the rising importance of digital content, and the uniting thread of the common standards—and stakeholders' struggles to bring it all together. I believe this story has a crucial moral for information professionals: Never before have we had such an opportunity to bring our unique expertise to the success of the important activities of teaching and learning. As librarians, the story is *ours* to tell.

This book would not have been possible without Glenn Sobey, who literally opened the door to the STEM school library; Dr. Ellen Hoffman, who opened it even wider; the late Dr. Chuck Achilles who gave me the tools to help me understand what I was seeing; Dr. Lee Zia, who gave me a chance; Dr. Kaye Howe, who kept giving me a chance; Dr. Anne Perrault, who keeps me inspired and sane; my dear friends in the NSDL community who, after 15 years, have become my family; Casey McLaughin and Michael "Wabi" Wabiszewski who translated my vision for better tools into reality; and my wonderful husband Glenn Rainey, who patiently listens and supports me through early mornings and late nights. Thank you everyone.

CHAPTER 1

Introduction

Introduction

The collection is at the core. It's at the center of everything we do as information professionals, and developing it is the unique role that school librarians play within the learning community. With a specific focus on open digital multimedia learning resources, this book is designed to help school librarians build, evaluate, and maintain their libraries' science, technology, engineering, and mathematics (STEM) collections to help learners work toward mastery of the Common Core State Standards (CCSS) in mathematics and interdisciplinary reading, and the Next Generation Science Standards (NGSS). Its aim is to provide a resource that:

- Helps librarians understand the nature and importance of STEM as well as of including high-quality, free STEM digital multimedia in library collections;

- Guides librarians through a collection analysis to determine the age and extent of their STEM collections, and define priorities for enriching collections with STEM digital multimedia resources;

- Gives librarians criteria and sources with which to build STEM collections that meet national standards for science (including health), technology, engineering, and mathematics. The scope of the proposed book is Dewey classes 000, 500, and 600, although some attention is given to resources that cross curriculum areas;

- Shows school librarians techniques for describing and classifying resources, with additional classification guidance regarding alignment to the CCSS and the NGSS; and

- Presents strategies for promoting collections to learners, educators, parents, community members, and—importantly—other school librarians.

Defining Terms and Frameworks

Before proceeding, let's stop here and introduce the terms you'll see frequently. Although this is not an attempt to have exhaustive definitions for each of the terms lists, the sections below describe how they can be defined.

Curation

Although there many competing definitions of curation, the one that resonates most strongly with me—and the one I had in mind when writing this book—comes from entrepreneur Steven Rosenbaum in his recent book *Curation Nation*.

> Curation . . . comes in many shapes and sizes. It is critically important to understand two things. First curation is about adding value from humans who add their qualitative judgment to whatever is being gathered and organized. And second, there is both amateur and professional curation, and the emergence of amateur or pro-sumer curators isn't in any way a threat to professionals. (Rosenbaum 2011, 3–4)

As information professionals, librarians function in the role of professional curators. Librarians are also attuned to building a collection that meets the needs and interests of their learning communities, however, often fielding suggestions and recommendations of the "prosumers" (PROfessional conSUMERs).

Educational Digital Library

In 2003, a number of definitions of digital library were synthesized and then distilled in the context of education.

> An educational digital library is minimally composed of 1) Linked collections of learning objects accessible from a variety of [online]

points; 2) Descriptions for objects and collections beyond author, title, and location; 3) Services that add value to the collections and objects; [and] 4) Additional features, such as community-building mechanisms, that cannot be represented or distributed in print formats. (Mardis 2003, 1–2)

Empowering Learners' Roles

As the predominant professional association for school librarians in the United States, the American Association of School Librarians (AASL) provides professional guidelines and learning standards to guide professionals' practice. *Empowering Learners* (AASL 2009a) is AASL's most current set of professional guidelines. The guidelines articulate five roles for school librarians.

- As a **leader**, the school librarian helps all members of the learning environment to value and develop twenty-first century learning skills. A school librarian who is a leader serves as both a teacher and a learner—listening to and acting upon good ideas from peers, teachers, and students. School librarian leaders have a strong professional commitment and a thorough knowledge of the challenges and opportunities facing their profession. They are active members of the local and global learning community, and build relationships with organizations and stakeholders to develop effective school library media programs and advocate for student learning.

- As a **teacher**, the school librarian collaborates with students and other members of the learning community to analyze learning and information needs, to locate and use resources that meet those needs, and to understand and communicate the information the resources provide. As effective instructors, school librarians stay up to date with current research on teaching and learning and apply its findings to a variety of situations—particularly those that call upon students to access, evaluate, and use information from multiple sources to learn, to think, and to create and apply new knowledge. A curriculum leader and a full participant on the instructional team, the school librarian constantly updates personal skills and knowledge to work effectively with teachers, administrators, and other staff members— both to expand their general understanding of information issues, and to provide specific opportunities to develop sophisticated skills in information literacy, including the uses of information technology.

- As an **instructional partner**, the school librarian joins with teachers and others to identify links across student information needs, curricular content, learning outcomes, and the wide variety of print, non-print, and electronic information resources. Working with the entire school community, the school librarian takes a leading role in developing policies, practices, and curricula that guide students in developing a full range of information and communication abilities. Committed to the process of collaboration, the school librarian works closely with individual teachers in the critical areas of designing authentic learning tasks and assessments and integrating the information and communication abilities required to meet subject-matter standards.

- As an **information specialist**, the school librarian provides leadership and expertise in acquiring and evaluating information resources in all formats; in bringing an awareness of information issues into collaborative relationships with teachers, administrators, students, and others; and in modeling for students and others strategies for locating, accessing, and evaluating information within and beyond the library media center. Working in an environment that has been profoundly affected by technology, the school librarian both masters sophisticated electronic resources and maintains a constant focus on the nature, quality, and ethical use of information available in these and in more traditional tools.

- As a **program administrator**, the school librarian works collaboratively with members of the learning community to define the policies of the library media program and to guide and direct all activities related to it. Confident in the importance of the effective use of information and information technology to students' personal and economic success in their futures, the school librarian is an advocate for the school library media program and provides the knowledge, vision, and leadership to steer it creatively and energetically in the twenty-first century. Proficient in the management of staff, budgets, equipment, and facilities, the school librarian plans, executes, and evaluates the program to ensure its quality both at a general level and on a day-to-day basis. (Adapted from AASL 2009a, 17–18)

Granularity

Think of granularity in terms of a grain of sand. A single grain of sand is the smallest unit and a beach is a much larger unit. The same concept applies to learning objects. A "chapter" section from a video or a single image represents a very small level of granularity, a lesson plan represents a mid-sized level of granularity, and a course module represents a much larger level. For an illustration of this idea, see Chapter 4.

Learning Objects

A pioneering promoter of online learning, Brigham Young University professor David Wiley defined learning objects as described below.

> Learning objects are elements of a new type of computer-based instruction grounded in the object-oriented paradigm of computer science. . . . [T]he fundamental idea behind learning objects [is that] instructional designers can build small (relative to the size of an entire course) instructional components that can be reused a number of times in different learning contexts. Additionally, learning objects are generally understood to be digital entities deliverable over the Internet, meaning that any number of people can access and use them simultaneously (as opposed to traditional instructional media, such as an overhead or videotape, which can only exist in one place at a time). Moreover, those who incorporate learning objects can collaborate on and benefit immediately from new versions. These are significant differences between learning objects and other instructional media that have existed previously. (Wiley 2000, p. 3)

Learning objects can be free or can have a cost associated with them; they could be created by corporate entities or individuals. They can be editable or static.

Machine Readable Cataloging Records

Machine readable cataloging (MARC) records are digital versions of catalog records that contain descriptive information for library resources. The MARC record format is the current standard for library resources.

Metadata

Literally, metadata are data about data. A metadata record describes an information resource. MARC is an example of a metadata record.

Online Public Access Catalog

Also called "library management systems" (LMS), online public access catalog (OPAC) refers to online card catalogs that contain metadata in MARC format.

Open Educational Resources

The Hewlett Foundation defines open educational resources (OER) below.

> [Open educational resources are] teaching, learning, and research resources that reside in the public domain or have been released under an intellectual property license that permits their free use and re-purposing by others. [OER] include full courses, course materials, modules, textbooks, streaming videos, tests, software, and any other tools, materials, or techniques used to support access to knowledge. (Hewlett Foundation, 2014, para. 3)

Every OER is a learning object, but not every learning object is an OER. Open educational resources use licenses (e.g., Creative Commons licenses) that permit reuse, editing, and remixing. Some learning objects can have restrictions and costs associated with use.

Digital Resources and the School Librarian: An Overview

Myriad educational digital library (EDL) projects have exemplary collections for elementary and secondary educators and students. The prevalence of digital media available in these collections offers new opportunities to diversify school library collections with "open educational resources": downloadable and editable digital video and audio, data sets, interactives, simulations, and hypertext resources. If you encounter an unfamiliar term, simply check the handy list of definitions provided above.

Many of these projects offer workshops to enable rich implementation of the available resources. A key actor not targeted by many digital library projects is the school librarian. Despite these efforts, school use of digital open educational resources remains nascent. Results of prior research devoted to examining the implementation process has suggested that to achieve deep and lasting digital library content integration in schools, support beyond professional development is needed and school-based actors beyond students and classroom teachers must be included. Librarians need to know more about the complications inherent in the process of integrating open content in school library activities.

STEM and the School Librarian: An Overview

Readers might notice that the title of this book contains the term "STEM." Although the role of school librarians in enhancing their collections with OER might seem like an obvious development, for many librarians, their crucial role in science, technology, engineering, and mathematics (STEM) learning is less apparent. In the 15 years spent researching the intersection between STEM and libraries, my investigations have revealed the unrealized potential for enhancing STEM curriculum through school librarians and STEM teacher collaboration based on school library resources. School librarians have a 1:65 ratio to classroom teachers in U.S. schools (National Center for Education Statistics 2014), and provide a virtually untapped source of local expertise for the dissemination of, and instructional support for, digital open-content resources and techniques that can have a direct positive relationship with STEM teaching and student learning.

In many ways, STEM classrooms and school libraries are struggling with common reform issues and with documenting their positive impacts within school systems. Nationally, educational policy makers point to faltering STEM reform initiatives and low test scores as trends that culminate in a population that is illiterate in science and with few students pursuing STEM careers (Committee on STEM Education, National Science and Technology Council 2013; National Science Board [NSB] 2014). As pressures to expand data-driven decisions in schools increase, every component of the learning environment must show a demonstrable effect. Yet, STEM leaders (e.g., the National Science Teachers' Association, the American Association for the Advancement of Science) are not on record recognizing the contributions that school librarians could make in support of their improvement efforts (Lance, Rodney, and Hamilton-Pennell 2000; Valenza 2007). School librarians also do not seem to be effective in building needed relationships with STEM educators in a widespread manner (Harris 2006).

Bringing STEM Digital Resources to the School Library: An Overview

As readers might know, librarians play many roles in learning. A unique and primary role, however, is building and maintaining a resource base for teaching and learning. School librarians locate and organize materials that support the curriculum and student interests, and make them findable through instructional collaboration and the Online Public Access

Catalog (OPAC), today's card catalog. With the advent of the first OPACs in the mid-1970s, libraries started to replace traditional card catalogs (Nisonger 2000). Librarians, in essence, began building and maintaining their own vast metadata repositories that included bibliographic information, with features like holdings information and request services (Okerson 2000). Traditionally, OPACs have pointed only to physical resources, but they have the technical capacity to include records that point to a range of media. OPACs thus are a building block for greater distribution and increased awareness of open content.

We should not assume that all librarians know how to leverage their resource expertise and collaborative roles to foster engaged learning through open educational resources. Recent studies have shown that, although many students best learn STEM concepts with OER, few teachers infuse it into practice (Kay and Knaack 2007; Recker et al. 2007). School librarians are the catalyst needed for teachers and students to engage in innovative learning.

Guided by the overarching question "How can school libraries support strong STEM achievement with digital library open content?" this book aims to explore ways in which a school librarian can use open educational resources to expand and enrich the school library's resource base and instructional support. It provides a framework for school librarians to promote sustainable open content use in schools.

Who Is This Book's Target?

In an effort to increase the integration of digital open content and physical STEM resources, enhance their findability, and promote their use in teaching and learning, this book is designed to meet the needs of numerous audiences.

- School librarians can benefit from this book immediately. It provides information regarding the use of open educational resources to support STEM in school library collections and gives strategies to work closely with STEM teachers and students to access the open educational resources for STEM classroom use.
- Public librarians will gain insight and ideas for informal learning programs and collection strategies that engage the public and augment the collection in affordable, high-quality ways.
- Teachers will benefit from this proposal by working with school librarians to integrate open content into teaching.

- Library and information studies (LIS) students will experience greater motivation in learning through the use of open content and its exciting technology-mediated applications.
- Open educational resource providers will gain access to information about audiences and markets that is not reported elsewhere.

Although the availability of OER is growing, never before have the issues centered on research and practice with digital STEM resource. This book can help resources librarians who now must participate in the shift to digital learning and its emphasis on STEM learning.

Summary of Chapters

Although no text can include everything there is to know about a topic, the assembled chapters are based on topics that should provide readers with a sound understanding of some key topics and introduce key sources, tools, and techniques.

Chapter 2. STEM Is Important to Librarians

This chapter explores the policy and practice of the STEM field and its learning emphases in the context of school librarians' roles and areas of expertise. It also looks at the evidence showing that school librarians can provide unique and powerful support for STEM learning and teaching.

Chapter 3. The Common Standards Movement Is Important for School Librarians

This chapter traces the history of the common standards movement, explores the motivations behind the CCSS and NGSS, probes current controversies about the standards, and links the common standards movement to STEM learning and OER.

Chapter 4. Curation Part 1: Selecting and Describing STEM Digital Resources

The STEM resources present their own special considerations for selection and description, especially when they're linked to standards. This chapter explores tips, tools, and techniques for STEM OERs.

Chapter 5. Curation Part 2: Managing and Promoting Your STEM OER Collection

Once the collection is built, how do you promote its use and keep it fresh? This chapter looks at strategies linked to *Empowering Learners'* (AASL 2009a) roles and the AASL *Standards for the 21st Century Learner* (AASL 2009b) for school librarians.

Chapter 6. Summary and Conclusion: An Open Letter to School Librarians and Science Educators

This chapter reflects on the many ways librarians can lead with their collection through the integration of STEM open content linked to the common standards.

Each chapter begins with an overview, describes key research and policy, presents best practices from librarianship, and features tools and techniques to help you get started.

CHAPTER 2

STEM Is Important to Librarians

Chapter Highlights

- Historical importance of STEM
- Current STEM policy perspectives
- STEM learning and teaching
- STEM and school libraries

The health and longevity of our Nation's citizenry, economy and environmental resources depend in large part on the acceleration of scientific and technological innovations, such as those that improve health care, inspire new industries, protect the environment, and safeguard us from harm. Maintaining America's historical preeminence in the STEM fields will require a concerted and inclusive effort to ensure that the STEM workforce is equipped with the skills and training needed to excel in these fields.

—John P. Holdren, Assistant to the President
for Science & Technology, Director,
Office of Science and Technology Policy

Introduction

Two events in American history astounded the science world more than any other events. Fifteen years after the Pearl Harbor attack, the former Union of Soviet Socialist Republics (USSR) launched the first artificial satellite. *Sputnik* launched on October 4, 1957, jump-starting American educational reform and initiating the federal government's long-reaching foray into American education (National Academy of Education [NAE] 2009).

Bill Colglazier of the National Academy of Sciences commented, "One of the ironies of the *Sputnik* phenomenon is that America's paranoia about its technological gap led to a 'first renaissance' in science education" (Boyle 1997). A race to space could only be supported by a workforce fluent in science, technology, engineering, and mathematics (STEM). President Eisenhower signed the National Defense Education Act (NDEA) into law in 1958, providing the nation with sweeping legislation to codify the national preoccupation with science—and providing school librarians with their first source of federal support for building science and mathematics collections. *Sputnik* fueled changes in science curriculum, materials, and standards that were intended to ensure that American students were prepared for careers in science and technology.

Whether the United States won or is still leading the STEM-based space race is unclear. Compared to other industrialized countries, U.S. students tend to fare poorly on international measures of science and mathematics (National Science Board [NSB] 2006, 2008, 2014). One test, the Programme for International Assessment (PISA) measures the acquired knowledge and skills of students nearing the completion of their high school careers in the areas of science and mathematics literacy, reading, and problem solving (OECD 2010). The 2012 PISA revealed that among the 34 OECD countries, the United States performed below average in mathematics and near average in reading and science. These scores have placed American students twenty-first out of 30 industrialized nations in science and twenty-fifth of 30 industrialized nations in math (Organisation for Economic Cooperation and Development [OECD] 2014). Equally disturbing is the National Assessment of Educational Progress (NAEP) which revealed minimal gains in mathematics for eighth graders and stagnant growth for fourth graders (National Center for Education Statistics 2013). The trend toward declining test scores in math and science has raised the alarm that the present generation of students will be ill-prepared to meet the challenges of a global society and faltering economy (National Academy of Education [NAE] 2009).

This chapter explores the connection between STEM and school libraries through an examination of federal education policy initiatives, best practices in STEM learning and teaching, leadership focuses for school librarians, and how these forces blend together to create a unique and timely opportunity for information professionals in educational organizations.

STEM in the Policy Spotlight

Spurred by the unfavorable international comparisons, education policymakers are scrutinizing how science is learned and taught in American schools, and this examination calls into question the role of digital resources and technology in improving STEM achievement. STEM is again the focus of a renewed emphasis and federal funding. During President Barack Obama's first term, the administration used multiple strategies to make progress on improving STEM education.

- The first round of the Department of Education's $4.3 billion "Race to the Top" competition offered states a competitive preference priority for developing comprehensive strategies to improve achievement and provide rigorous curricula in STEM subjects; partner with local STEM institutions, businesses, and museums; and broaden participation of women and girls and other groups underrepresented in STEM fields.

- President Obama announced the goal to prepare 100,000 excellent STEM teachers over the next decade in his 2011 State of the Union Address.

- The president hosted the first-ever White House Science Fair in late 2010 and the second in 2012, fulfilling a commitment he made at the launch of his "Educate to Innovate" campaign to directly use his bully pulpit to inspire more boys and girls to excel in mathematics and science. The president also issued a call to action to the 200,000 federal scientists and engineers to volunteer in their local communities and think of creative ways to engage students in STEM subjects (Committee on STEM Education, National Science and Technology Council 2013, iii–iv).

In addition to the National Science Foundation (NSF) and Department of Education (ED), the Department of Commerce (DOC), Department of Energy (DOE), the Department of the Interior (DOI), Department of Defense (DOD), the National Aeronautics and Space Administration (NASA), and the U.S. Department of Agriculture (USDA) also have statutory responsibility to provide STEM education. Although only a small fraction of the ED's funding supports specific STEM education programs, STEM initiatives have been a competitive priority in such significant programs as "Race to the Top" (RT3). The RT3 competitive state grant program has infused more than $6 billion into states' attempts to improve teaching and learning (U.S. Department of Education 2014).

What Is Science Learning?

The National Research Council's *Taking Science to School* report (Duschl, Schweingruber, and Shouse 2007) concluded that science learning requires students to engage in a range of experiences or practices. As condensed from the subsequent *Framework for Science Learning* (Quinn, Schweingruber, and Keller 2012, 251–52), experiences can be categorized into the following four strands.

- Strand 1. Knowing, using, and interpreting scientific explanations of the natural world. This strand includes the acquisition of facts, laws, principles, theories, and models of science; the development of conceptual structures that incorporate them; and the productive use of these structures to understand the natural world.

- Strand 2. Generating and evaluating scientific evidence and explanations. This strand encompasses the knowledge and practices needed to build and refine models and to provide explanations (conceptual, computational, and mechanistic) based on scientific evidence.

- Strand 3. Understanding the nature and development of scientific knowledge. Strand 3 focuses on students' understanding of science as a way of knowing. . . . [Students] come to appreciate that alternative interpretations of scientific evidence can occur, that such interpretations must be carefully scrutinized, and that the plausibility of the supporting evidence must be considered. . . . [S]tudents ultimately understand regarding both their own work and the historical record that predictions or explanations can be revised on the basis of seeing new evidence, or of developing a new model that accounts for the existing evidence better than previous models did.

- Strand 4. Participating productively in scientific practices and discourse. Strand 4 includes students' effective engagement in science practices with an understanding of the norms for participating in science, such as norms for constructing and presenting scientific models and explanations, for critiquing and defending a claim while engaged in scientific debates, and for students' motivation and attitudes toward science. . . . Students come to see themselves as members of a scientific community in which they test ideas, develop shared representations and models, and reach consensus. . . . [Students learn to] believe that steady effort in understanding science pays off—as opposed to erroneously thinking that some people understand science and other people never will.

The four strands provide a high-level science learning framework that rests on an interconnected and social system of thought, discourse, and practice. The strands stress the ability to develop explanations of phenomena and to carry out empirical investigations to develop or evaluate those knowledge claims, as well as for students' conceptions of the world to be modified as they learn science. These strands are mutually supportive—students' advances in one strand tend to leverage or promote advances in other strands. Further, students use them together when engaging in scientific tasks (Subramaniam et al. 2013).

Libraries, Librarians, and STEM Learning

The potential for positive relationships in student engagement and achievement through school library collections and from school librarian–teacher collaboration are demonstrated in many previous studies (e.g., Francis, Lance, and Leitzau 2010; Scholastic 2008). Whether in the United States, Canada, Australia, or other locations, researchers consistently have concluded that student reading test scores had a statistically significant positive correlation with many specific features of school libraries.

Building on these studies, the relationship between science test scores and aspects of school library facilities, programs, and professionals was studied (Mardis 2005, 2007). My study replicated the statistical analyses of earlier studies with the input of focus group interactions. The findings indicated that many aspects of school library collection and services had a strong positive relationship to higher science test scores even when major predictive factors of student achievement such as district minority enrollment, socioeconomic status, and per-pupil expenditure were taken into account.

As noted, the 1958 NDEA was the first incidence of federal support for the purchase of school library materials. This legislation established clearly that the school library collection played an instrumental role in science learning. It is safe to assume that we can interpret this relationship to signal a collection cultivated by a trained school librarian. The information specialist role has been present in school librarian professional standards since their advent (Mardis 2006a). In the recent past, the *Information Power* (AASL and AECT 1998) professional standards were revised and expanded to reflect the explosion of knowledge made possible by advances in information technology in schools and the increased opportunities access brings to the school library media program.

Three themes for practice are established in *Information Power* (AASL and AECT 1998) and echoed in the most recent guidelines, *Empowering Learners* (AASL 2009a): collaboration, leadership, and technology. The collaborative theme recognizes the influence of collaborative teaching on student achievement (Lange, Magee, and Montgomery 2003); the leadership theme recognizes that steady and visionary leadership is widely evident in effective school media programs (Lance and Loertscher 2001); the technology role recognizes that access to and facility with information technology is essential (Kuhlthau 1997). Often, discussions about the school library are treated as synonymous with discussions of educational technology, because the library often is the location of the majority of the school's technology equipment (Lance and Loertscher 2001). Technology, however, merely is a vehicle for information seeking, creation, and communication.

School librarian practitioners and scholarly literature rarely address support of science achievement (Mardis 2006b), yet both science teachers and school librarians are struggling with increasing curriculum pressures and with documenting their own positive effects on student learning. As the trend toward data-driven decision making grows in the school setting, it is increasingly important for every component of the learning environment to have demonstrable effect and to be mutually reinforcing. Still, science reformers do not address the potential for school librarians to support their efforts nor do school library practitioners and researchers seem to be focusing on building relationships with science educators (Lanahan 2002).

Science education includes many integrated components that are compatible with principles and common practices in school library programs. Science education and school library programs have practical and philosophical commonalities that justify exploring their link. A comparison of science and AASL's school library learning framework, the *Standards for the 21ˢᵗ Century Learner* (AASL 2009b) reveals a number of congruences. Researchers from within and beyond school librarianship (Subramaniam et al. 2013) likewise have noted the similarities depicted in Figure 2.1.

As Figure 2.1 depicts, both literacies require learners to be able to identify a problem, systematically investigate the problem by gathering information, and assess the problem with the gathered information. The

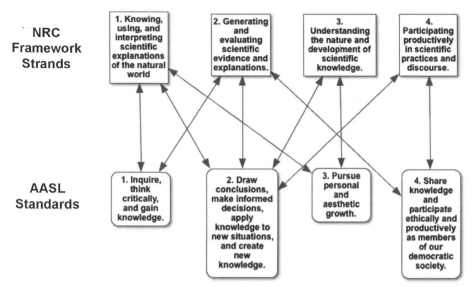

NRC Framework Strands

| 1. Knowing, using, and interpreting scientific explanations of the natural world | 2. Generating and evaluating scientific evidence and explanations. | 3. Understanding the nature and development of scientific knowledge. | 4. Participating productively in scientific practices and discourse. |

AASL Standards

| 1. Inquire, think critically, and gain knowledge. | 2. Draw conclusions, make informed decisions, apply knowledge to new situations, and create new knowledge. | 3. Pursue personal and aesthetic growth. | 4. Share knowledge and participate ethically and productively as members of our democratic society. |

Figure 2.1. Comparison of NRC (2007) strands and AASL (2007) learning standards.

vision of both sets of guidelines is to promote research-based contemporary learning theories. Both AASL's *Standards* and the NRC *Framework for K–12 Science Education* emphasize that the active building of knowledge through construction and inquiry is the key to the authentic learning that modern education seeks to promote.

Both sets of guidelines are founded on an idea of literacy. The AASL defines information literacy as "the ability to recognize when information is needed and have the ability to locate, evaluate, and use effectively the needed information" (AASL and AECT 1998) and emphasizes the need for multiple literacies. According to the National Science Education Standards (NSES):

> Scientific literacy is the knowledge and understanding of scientific concepts and processes required for personal decision making, participation in civic and cultural affairs, and economic productivity. People who are scientifically literate can ask for, find, or determine answers to questions about everyday experiences. They are able to describe, explain, and predict natural phenomena. (NRC 1996, 1)

In many educational organizations, the relationship between science education and school library programs has attained a "chicken or the egg"–type of cycle: Science teachers do not often use the school library because they do not feel that the school librarian has the resources or the skills to help them; the school librarian might not choose or develop the skills or resources to help science educators because they are not frequent users of the school library program (Mardis 2007).

Reinforcing Aspects of Science Teaching and School Librarianship

An examination of the professional guidelines for both science teachers and school librarians also suggests that, despite the lack of current cooperation, these roles arise from similar beliefs about the school community and student learning.

In an effort to give science teachers—with their diverse backgrounds and experiences—a common language, multiple efforts have been undertaken to create instructional guidelines and goals. Despite the spread of new national science and mathematics learning standards, STEM teaching standards are well established and new professional standards have not yet been released. The American Association for the Advancement of Science (AAAS) established Project 2061 (AAAS 1990), a long-term initiative to improve science literacy, and the National Science Teachers Association (NSTA) contributed to benchmarking and dissemination efforts. Finally, in 1996, the National Research Council (NRC) unified the AAAS and NSTA efforts into the National Science Education Standards. These standards proceed from a belief in high student expectations, teaching for depth of understanding, science literacy, and active learning; the NSES recognize that diversity in approaches and perspectives will exist within its framework (Ellis 2003). The standards also strongly promote professional development to increase awareness of different teaching and learning ideas.

The National Science Teaching Standards—the portion of the National Science Education Standards that addresses classroom practice—begin with encouraging teachers to develop a long-term plan for science teaching that facilitates inquiry-based learning, includes formative and summative assessments, and creates a conducive physical setting (NRC 1996). Although the imperative to balance and integrate immediate demands (such as state-mandated standardized tests) with professional standards is an ongoing challenge, the National Science Teaching Standards give educators a lens through which to examine their own practice as well as their role in the school community.

An overview of the roles and their mutually reinforcing nature is depicted in Figure 2.2. Each of the National Science Teaching

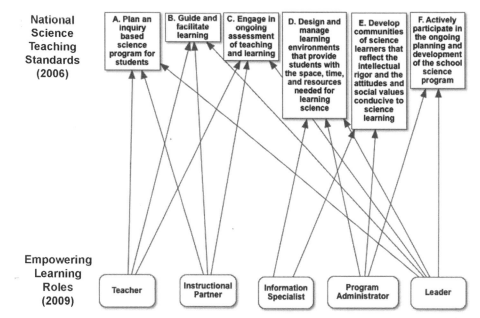

Figure 2.2. Mutually reinforcing roles as defined by national science teacher and school librarian standards.

Standards is delineated across the top of the figure; each of the *Empowering Learners* roles is listed across the bottom of the figure.

Figure 2.2 reflects that the roles of science teachers and of school librarians enjoy a fair amount of commonality. Depending upon the school context in which these educators work, the overlap can be even greater. These relationships are described in more detail below. Within each of these sets of guidelines, activities for science teachers and school librarians are broken down into role elements.

Teaching Standard A

In Teaching Standard A, teachers of science are to plan inquiry-based science programs for their students. In doing this, teachers will develop a framework of yearlong and short-term goals for students; select science content and adapt and design curricula to meet the interests, knowledge, understanding, abilities, and experiences of students; select teaching and assessment strategies that support the development of student understanding and nurture a community of science learners; and work together as colleagues within and across disciplines and grade levels (NRC 1996).

Teaching Standard B

To meet Teaching Standard B, science teachers guide and facilitate learning. Teachers focus and support inquiries while interacting with students; orchestrate discourse among students about scientific ideas; challenge students to accept and share responsibility for their own learning; recognize and respond to student diversity and encourage all students to participate fully in science learning; and encourage and model the skills of scientific inquiry, as well as the curiosity, openness to new ideas and data, and skepticism that characterize science (NRC 1996).

Teachers often have to choose between preparing students for high-stakes tests, investing the extra planning time required by inquiry-based activities, and enacting NSES practices (Humphrey and Carver 1998). The school librarian might be able to provide crucial support to a teacher in this situation. In the "Teacher" role, the school librarian is knowledgeable about current research on teaching and learning and is skilled in applying its findings to a variety of situations. Librarians also work with students to access, evaluate, and use information from multiple sources to learn, to think, and to expand their general understanding of information issues (AASL 2009a). Especially using information technology, school librarians can help students learn how to effectively complete classroom tasks using school library resources. In the "Instructional Partner" role, the school librarian is committed to the process of collaboration (AASL 2009a). School librarians can share the burden of instructional planning and enable teachers to focus on instructional expertise.

Teaching Standard C

To address Teaching Standard C, teachers of science are to engage in ongoing assessment of their teaching and of student learning. In doing this, teachers should use multiple methods and systematically gather data about student understanding and ability; analyze assessment data to guide teaching; and guide students in self-assessment. Teachers should use student data, observations drawn from teaching, and interactions with colleagues to reflect on and improve their teaching practices. By using student data, observations of teaching, and interactions with colleagues, science teachers should be able to report student achievement and opportunities to learn to students, teachers, parents, policymakers, and the general public (NRC 1996).

Student assessment also is an area in which the school librarian has expertise. In the "Teacher" role, the school librarian collaborates with members of the learning community to analyze learning and information needs, to locate and use resources that meet those needs, and to understand and communicate the information the resources provide (AASL 2009a). By interacting with the school librarian to discuss information needs, subject areas, and activities that require resource support, teachers can reflect on their own practices and identify possible solutions to student learning problems.

In the "Instructional Partner" role, the school librarian works closely with individual teachers in the critical areas of designing authentic learning tasks and assessments and integrating the information and communication abilities required to meet subject-matter standards (AASL 2009a). With the assistance of the school librarian, teachers can undertake more informal and observational assessment techniques as well as work in collaboration with media specialists to perform assessment activities. This cooperation can improve the quality of assessment by including multiple viewpoints and by providing external validation of instruments.

Teaching Standard D

To meet Teaching Standard D, science teachers design and manage learning environments that provide students with the time, space, and resources needed for learning science. In doing this, teachers structure the time available so that students are able to engage in extended investigations; create a setting for student work that is flexible and supportive of science inquiry; ensure a safe working environment; make the available science tools, materials, media, and technological resources accessible to students; identify and use resources outside the school; engage students in designing the learning environment; and develop environments that enable students to learn science (NRC 1996).

In the "Information Specialist" role, the school librarian provides leadership and expertise in acquiring and evaluating information resources in all formats, and in modeling for students and others strategies for locating, accessing, and evaluating information within and beyond the school librarian (AASL 2009a). School librarians can form critical links not only to resources held by the school librarian, but also to informal learning contexts such as museums and zoos and to experts and mentors in the community and available via the Internet.

These recommendations are in line with the fact that many middle school students—especially those with learning challenges—reported that learning science with the aid of a variety of resources, such as those found in the school library collection, is very important (Lee 2005; Lemke 2000). The reading skills honed in the library through exposure to informational text and pleasure reading also support science learning. School library programs that focus on the continuing cultivation of literacy at the secondary level are able to give students the strong reading skills that have been found to compensate for deficits in student science content knowledge and enable quick acquisition of conceptual knowledge. Moreover, students who are able to locate and comprehend scholarly articles are able to apply scientific models to deepen and improve their active science learning (Windschitl and Thompson 2006). In these ways, reading acts as a keystone skill for learning that also relies upon the location, selection, and synthesis of information for maximum impact. This combination of skills, when applied to science learning, has the greatest relationship with science achievement on high-stakes standardized tests (O'Reilly and McNamara 2007).

Teaching Standard E

Teaching Standard E states that teachers of science are to develop communities of science learners that reflect the intellectual rigor of scientific inquiry and the attitudes and social values conducive to science learning. In doing this, teachers display and demand respect for the diverse ideas, skills, and experiences of all students; enable students to have a significant voice in decisions about the content and context of their work, and require students to take responsibility for the learning of all members of the community; nurture collaboration among students; structure and facilitate ongoing formal and informal discussion based on a shared understanding of rules of scientific discourse; and model and emphasize the skills, attitudes, and values of scientific inquiry (NRC 1996).

As an "Instructional Partner," the school librarian leads the development of policies, practices, and curricula that guide students to develop the full range of information and communication abilities (AASL and AECT 1998). In this role, the school librarian can promote resource evaluation and the ethical use of information. Students can learn not just what information is available to them, but how to judge its quality and its appropriateness for their needs.

As "Information Specialist," the school librarian has a mastery of sophisticated electronic resources, and maintains a constant focus on the nature, quality, and ethical use of information available in these and in more traditional tools (AASL and AECT 1998). With the aid of the school librarian, students can learn when to refer to print resources and when to use electronic sources, as well as how to locate information in these resources quickly and effectively. With the use of digital libraries and other online community-building and research tools, school librarians can provide access to unique tools that support the inquiry process and promote principles of investigation, analysis, and critical literacy (Bell 2004).

Teaching Standard F

To meet Teaching Standard F, teachers of science are to actively participate in the ongoing planning and development of the school science program. In doing this, teachers plan and develop the school science program; participate in decisions concerning the allocation of time and other resources to the science program; and participate fully in planning and implementing professional growth and development strategies for themselves and their colleagues (NRC 1996).

In the "Instructional Partner" role, the school librarian joins with teachers and others to identify links across student information needs and curricular content (AASL and AECT 1996). With an overall view of the curriculum, school librarians are well positioned to help science teachers identify activities in other curricular areas that provide complement and reinforcement to their students' learning.

A barrier to standards-based teaching is the difficulty teachers face in locating and managing instructional materials (Hoffman and Mardis 2008; Weiss et al. 2001). As a "Program Administrator," the school librarian works collaboratively with members of the learning community to define the policies of the library program, and to guide and direct all activities related to it (AASL 2009a). The school library's ability to support the science program with adequate resources depends on the strength of communication between the school librarian and the science teacher. This communication can ensure that an adequate budget is earmarked for learning resources, programs, and other activities.

Figure 2.2 does not explicitly include mathematics teaching. Mathematics is a key part of STEM and also a difficult point of intersection for school librarians. The 2014 National Council of Teachers of Mathematics (NCTM) professional standards in mathematics, however, appear to share many effective teaching practices with broader science teacher and school librarian instructional guidelines.

To summarize, NCTM's 2014 professional standards encourage teachers to guide their instruction and choice of learning activities with clear goals that foster a logical progression of mathematical learning through problem solving and reasoning. Effective mathematics teachers build procedural fluency and actively engage students in discussion, questioning, representation, and discourse. This helps students build and demonstrate their understanding through multiple contextual opportunities to flexibly solve contextual and mathematical problems. Although the NCTM (NCTM 2014, 7) teaching standards predominantly recall the teacher and information specialist roles, the leader role is woven throughout.

Barriers to Connecting

Teaching philosophy influences instructional practice, but other forces such as teacher preparedness and pre-service teacher education affect the classroom environment. Teachers at all levels report feeling unprepared to teach life, earth, or physical science, with elementary teachers at a particular disadvantage (Blank and Toye 2007; Horizon Research Inc. 2002; National Council on Teacher Quality 2014; Weiss et al. 2001). Pre-service science teachers also are not uniformly receiving the exposure to science teaching methods and approaches that enable them to develop their own perspectives on teaching and learning (National Council on Teacher Quality 2014; National Science Board [NSB] 2010).

Although the potential exists for positive outcomes in school librarian–STEM teacher collaborations, previous research has identified barriers that remain. STEM teachers reported that their school libraries tended to have old and small collections to support their subjects, and that their school librarians did not seem fluent in science and mathematics topics (Mardis 2004). School librarian–focused studies by Mardis (Mardis 2005, 2007) pointed to a lack of school library–focused professional development in STEM as a barrier to closer work with STEM teachers and students. School librarians might not be permitted to attend professional development events because they are not considered teachers; are not welcomed on curriculum committees; and are not permitted to engage in tasks that leave the library unstaffed. A review of current practitioner literature also suggested that school librarians cannot gain knowledge from professional reading because all STEM topics represented less than 5% of professional literature content (Mardis 2006b).

Conclusion

Even when studies suggest a disconnect between STEM teachers and school librarians, librarians remained positive about the potential of collaboration and had anecdotal evidence of small successes. For those situations in which collaboration with STEM teachers was occurring on at least a minimal level, school librarian interactions with STEM teachers took place through information resource provision and teaching STEM students information skills needed to complete assignments. These interactions—with the school librarian primarily acting as a resource provider and a teacher of information skills—affirm more than a decade of previous findings (Drake 2007; Francis et al. 2010; Slygh 2000; Straessle 2000).

Empowering the school librarian to focus on current and dynamic sources of STEM information could well be the key to promoting those resources to STEM teachers and students and also to effective collaboration. Subsequent chapters look at tools and strategies to build these connections.

Taking It Further: Related Readings

Julien, H., and S. Barker. 2009. "How High-School Students Find and Evaluate Scientific Information: A Basis for Information Literacy Skills Development." *Library & Information Science Research* 31 (1): 12–17.

Mardis, M. A., and E. S. Hoffman. 2007. "School Library Factors Affecting Science Achievement. Paper presented at the American Educational Research Association, Chicago, April 10–12.

Mardis, M. A., and A.M. Perrault. 2007. "Examining the Information Behaviors of Educators to Inform a Model of Professional Exchange between Science Teachers and Library Media Specialists." Paper presented at the American Educational Research Association, Chicago, April 10–12.

Montiel-Overall, P., and K. Grimes. 2013. "Teachers and Librarians Collaborating on Inquiry-Based Science Instruction: A Longitudinal Study." *Library & Information Science Research* 35 (1): 41–53. doi: 10.1016/j.lisr.2012.08.002.

Perrault, A. M. 2007. "An Exploratory Study of Biology Teacher's Online Information Seeking Practices." *School Library Research* 10. http://www.ala.org/ala/aasl/aaslpubsandjournals/slmrb/slmrcontents/volume10/biology.htm.

Rawson, C. H. 2014. "Every Flower in the Garden: Collaboration between School Librarians and Science Teachers." *School Libraries Worldwide* 20 (1): 20–28. doi: 10.14265.20.1.003.

Schultz-Jones, B., and C. Ledbetter. 2009. "Building Relationships in the School Social Network: Science Teachers and School Library Media Specialists Report Key Dimensions." *School Libraries Worldwide* 15 (2): 23–48.

CHAPTER 3

The Common Standards Movement Is Important for School Librarians

Chapter Highlights

- History of the standards movement
- Common Core State Standards
- Next Generation Science Standards
- Common standards learning environments

Introduction

Our current curriculum standards are the result of a larger standards movement in the United States. Prompted by *A Nation at Risk* (United States National Commission on Excellence and United States Department of Education 1983); a 1989 governors' education summit regarding education goals for 2000; and several versions of federal legislation, every state pledged to develop its own academic standards for K–12 core curriculum (Carmichael et al. 2010). The education standards movement gained momentum with the Clinton administration's *Goals*

2000 education plan, and that momentum continues today with state-level standards prompted by the No Child Left Behind Act providing an imperative for K–12 curriculum development. Standards-based reform is by far the biggest issue in American K–12 education today, and has been since at least 1989, when the nation's governors met with President George H. W. Bush in Charlottesville, Virginia, to set national education goals (Finn, Petrilli, and Julian 2006).

The standards documents produced by various levels of local education associations (LEAs) and professional teaching associations represented the efforts of education stakeholders to communicate the content and skills necessary for student success. Standards often are written in the format of what students should "know" (content) and "be able to do" (skills and abilities) in particular grades. Standards began in the five core curriculum areas of history, science, mathematics, English/language arts, and geography, although some states later added other disciplines such as government (civics), economics, and technology.

Standards implementation efforts have always been fraught with complications. Approximately 10 years after the call for states to draft standards, their implementation processes were uneven, at best. The Fordham Foundation's *State of State Standards* report (Finn and Petrilli 2000) includes an analysis of the extent to which national standards had made their way into state curriculum frameworks. For the five core subject areas, most states fared poorly and received failing grades. The Fordham Foundation's second state standards survey (Finn, Petrilli, and Julian 2006) reported that, although most states had revised or replaced their standards in many subjects, academic standards were no better in content or execution in 2006 than they were in 2000. The average grade was still low.

More tellingly, the U.S. Department of Education was unable to establish a relationship between state standards and student achievement on standardized tests such as the National Assessment of Education Progress (NAEP) (National Center for Education Statistics [NCES] 2007). The state standards movement yielded a very mixed bag of standards having varying degrees of quality and similarity. Because no one could determine the true effect of the standards, the quest for comparability between states began.

Early attempts to fit the standards into the existing educational system were plagued by problems due to competing economic, social, political, and institutional pressures on school administrators, teachers, and parents. The *State of the Standards* surveys (Finn, Petrilli, and Julian 2006; Finn and Petrilli 2000) included analyses of the barriers to standards implementation. This closer look at each state's implementation revealed a rather common set of challenges. In many instances, education officials reported feeling that standards documents were a federal attempt to control the curriculum in schools at the local level. Moreover, educators reported that standardized emphasis on curriculum content did not fit well with the constructivist learning environments favored by teachers and promoted by national organizations such as National Council of Teachers of Mathematics (NCTM), National Science Teachers Association (NSTA), and the National Council of Teachers of English (NCTE).

Beyond that, educators were overwhelmed by the sheer volume of curriculum material contained in the corpus of state standards documents. Because many state standards were authored through committee, in many instances the group compromises resulted in material that was unrealistic to implement given the length of the school day and year; the availability of qualified teachers; and existing graduation requirements. Add in local politics and a lack of articulation between states and local school districts, and successful implementation was blocked from many directions (Finn, Petrilli, and Julian 2006).

Three states—Massachusetts, California, and Indiana—successfully implemented curriculum frameworks because educational leaders in those states supported it with funding for local districts; allowed external organizations such as companies and higher education institutions to review and endorse standards documents; and reflected a single agreed-upon ideological and pedagogical orientation in each curriculum area. The standards that emerged from these states were clear, jargon-free, and reflected a strong and consistent commitment to learning and teaching each curriculum area (Finn, Petrilli, and Julian 2006). The successes of these three states laid the foundation for national common standards.

The Common Core State Standards

Recognizing the value of and need for consistent learning goals across states, in 2009 the Council of Chief State Schools Officers (CCSSO) and state governors of the National Governors' Association (NGA) coordinated an effort to develop the Common Core State Standards (CCSS). Designed through collaboration among teachers, school chiefs, administrators, and other experts, the standards are intended to provide a clear and consistent framework for student learning. The CCSS is not a product of the U.S. Department of Education.

The current version of the CCSS is research and evidence based and internationally benchmarked. The standards aim to be understandable

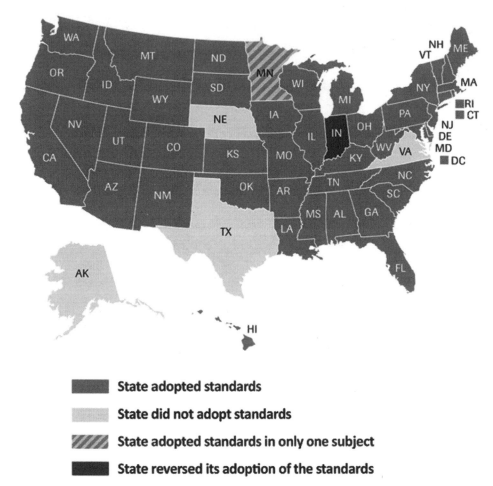

Figure 3.1. States' status for Common Core adoption as of October 2014.

and consistent, aligned with college and career expectations, and based on rigorous content and application of knowledge through higher-order thinking skills. The intent of the CCSS authors was to build upon the strengths and lessons of current state standards and look to other top-performing countries to determine how best to prepare all students for success in our global economy and society. To date, 45 states have adopted the CCSS, as Figure 3.1 illustrates. States now are focusing on implementation of the standards. Because it is a state-driven effort, implementation timelines vary.

The CCSS are based on the assumption that schools exist to develop competencies in children. The CCSS are expressed as contextual competencies but assume academic competence. Academic competence is what is considered to be traditional subject-area mastery; that is, individual competence in the procedures and factual recall within a specific discipline, such as the formula used to determine area in mathematics or spelling in English/language arts. Contextual competence, conversely, is based on collaborative work that allows students to infer and apply an appropriate range of interdisciplinary procedures and facts to solve problems or to express and defend a position. This competence might be expressed, for example, through using the formula for area to determine how much tile it requires to cover a floor. Knowledge of word stems might help a student determine the meaning of an unfamiliar word in a text. Both types of competencies are viewed as essential requirements for students to graduate from high school and be prepared to succeed in entry-level careers, introductory academic college courses, and workforce-training programs.

Instructional Shifts for the Common Core

The shift in emphasis from academic to contextual competence required a shift in instructional strategies. Table 3.1 provides an overview of these shifts in strategy.

English/language arts includes six main shifts in strategies. The first, "Balancing Informational and Literary Text," requires teachers to help students build competence with a range of texts including—but beyond—novels and short stories. Informational text includes nonfiction work and periodicals. Graphic novels are emphasized as important texts to bring into learning activities. The CCSS concludes with a special section focused on building textual literacy in a number of content areas, including science.

In "Building Knowledge in the Disciplines," students are asked to expand their understanding of the world through text. This shift is

Table 3.1. Instructional shifts in the Common Core

English/Language Arts	Mathematics
1. Balancing literary and informational text	1. Focus
2. Building knowledge in the disciplines	2. Coherence
3. Staircase of complexity	3. Fluency
4. Text-based answers	4. Deep understanding
5. Writing from sources	5. Applications
6. Academic vocabulary	6. Dual intensity

directly supported by the expanded use of informational text. To increase the "Staircase of Complexity," students are encouraged not just to read at grade level, but also to challenge themselves to read more-complex texts. Teachers are to provide the time, space, and support for this type of advanced reading. When teachers focus on "Text-Based Answers," students learn to use a variety of texts as evidence from which they synthesize content and construct answers to questions; with a focus on "Writing From Sources," students translate that use of evidence to persuasive writing in which they use evidence from texts to build and express arguments in a written format. Finally, when teachers "Increase Academic Vocabulary" through exposure to increasingly complex texts that are analyzed and synthesized for persuasion, students learn to understand and apply new vocabulary (Common Core State Standards Initiative [n.d.]-b).

The CCSS mathematics standards also call for instructional shifts that build and extend the NCTM processes of problem solving, reasoning and proof, communication, representation, and connections, and the NRC emphasis on adaptive reasoning, strategic competence, conceptual understanding, procedural fluency, and productive disposition. The CCSS mathematics standards have a new emphasis on application and "habitual inclination to see mathematics as sensible, useful, and worthwhile, coupled with a belief in diligence and one's own efficacy" (Common Core State Standards Initiative [n.d.]-a, 6).

The new mathematics standards include fewer topics but a more concentrated focus. Rather than racing to cover many topics in a "mile-wide, inch-deep curriculum" (Common Core State Standards Initiative [n.d.]-a, 3), the standards enable teachers to focus on helping students gain a solid understanding of concepts, a high degree of procedural skill and fluency, and the ability to apply the math they know to solve problems both inside and outside of the classroom. The standards also ask teachers to emphasize coherence by linking topics and thinking across grades so that students do not see mathematics as a list of disconnected topics. Teachers are asked to present mathematics as a coherent body of knowledge composed of interconnected concepts. This idea of coherence involves connecting mathematics work to ideas learning in prior grade levels and in other curriculum areas.

To help students meet the standards, educators must pursue—with equal intensity—three aspects of rigor in the major work of each grade: conceptual understanding, procedural skills and fluency, and application. Teachers should help students access concepts from a number of perspectives; build students' competence, calculation speed, and accuracy through practice; and help students to apply mathematics to problem solving (Common Core State Standards Initiative [n.d.]-c).

Common Core Controversies

Although states are not required to adopt the CCSS, 45 states signed on before the assessments even were created; some states are beginning to question that decision. Objections now arising include the cost of retooling tests, fears of government control over education, and concerns about states being compared to one another and penalized.

Education historian Diane Ravitch recently described the resistance to the CCSS as resulting from the extent to which states felt compelled to participate in the $5 billion federal "Race to the Top" program. In this program, states had to agree to evaluate teachers to a significant degree by student test scores; increase the number of privately managed charter schools; adopt "college and career–ready standards" (also known as the CCSS); take decisive action on low-performing schools by changing leadership or staff; and agree to collect, store, and share large amounts of personally identifiable student data (Strauss 2014).

Aside from states' concerns about the "Race to the Top" program, many states are questioning the cost of implementing the CCSS. States that adopt the CCSS must have an 85% degree of fidelity. Many states therefore are finding that the time and expertise required to perform this customization requires an investment beyond what they can afford (Bauerlein and Stotsky 2012). As a result, many states are adopting the online tests—PARCC and SmarterBalanced—which already are geared toward assessing college and career readiness. These tests are expensive, however, and also require significant technology and bandwidth expenditures (Strauss 2014).

Another driver of CCSS resistance is a lack of instructional materials that are explicitly linked to the standards (Jobrack 2012). Commercial textbooks have been found to be inadequate (Samuels 2012), and although the market potential for educational publishers is enormous (Mickey and Meaney 2013), many states and districts cannot afford to switch to a new textbook series and instead are turning to open educational resources (OER) as a cost-saving approach to accumulating sufficient educational content (Ash 2012). Even this approach is aspirational, however, because few state education leaders feel that they have access to the curatorial expertise required to ensure an appropriate supply of high-quality OER (National Science Digital Library [NSDL] 2013).

Next Generation Science Standards

Guided by the *NRC Framework* (presented in Chapter 2) and mirroring the CCSS, in July 2011 the Next Generation Science Standards (NGSS) were published. Created with input from a range of stakeholders including states, the National Research Council, the National Science Teachers Association, and the American Association for the Advancement of Science, this new set of standards aims to provide consistent science education through all grades, with an emphasis on engineering and technology. The NGSS describe what each student should know in the four domains of science—physical science; life science; earth and space science; and engineering, technology and science application. To date, 26 states have adopted the NGSS (Achieve, Inc. 2014). Those states are listed in Table 3.2.

As with the CCSS, the NGSS are focused on helping students become literate in applying scientific concepts and principles so that they will have the skills and knowledge to tackle real-world issues such as water quality and energy conservation. The NGSS are explicitly aligned to the Common Core State Standards so that when students are learning about science, they also are enhancing their skills in reading, writing, and math. Figure 3.2 depicts an example of an NGSS standard.

Table 3.2. States That Have Adopted the NGSS as of October 2014.

Arizona	Minnesota
Arkansas	Montana
California	New Jersey
Delaware	New York
Georgia	North Carolina
Illinois	Ohio
Iowa	Oregon
Kansas	Rhode Island
Kentucky	South Dakota
Maine	Tennessee
Maryland	Vermont
Massachusetts	Washington
Michigan	West Virginia

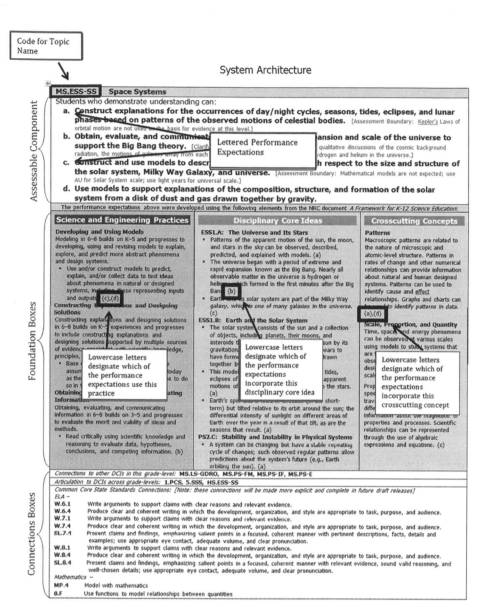

Figure 3.2. Sample Next Generation Science Standard.

As Figure 3.2 shows, within each disciplinary area the NGSS standards are internally organized and the framework is divided into three parts.

- Practices: Describe how scientists build theories and models about the way the world and systems within it work.

- Crosscutting concepts: Concepts that apply to all four science domains.

- Disciplinary core ideas: The foundational ideas needed for every student to be able to begin his or her own inquiries and practices.

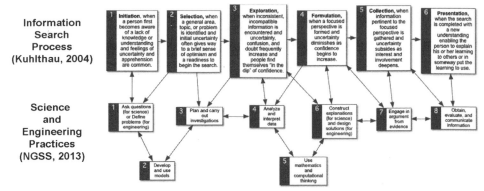

Figure 3.3. Links between the Information Search Process (Kuhlthau 2004) and Science and Engineering Practices (NGSS 2013).

Each standard begins with performance expectations and provides links between those performance expectations and aspects of each of science and engineering practices, disciplinary core areas, and crosscutting concepts. Each standard concludes with links to specific mathematics and ELA CCSS elements. The NGSS has been lauded for this construction based on the individual performance expectation and its built-in implementation support that links the CCSS to the NGSS. Even on an implementation level, "doing" science and "doing" information searching have an enormous amount of congruence, as Figure 3.3 shows.

Kuhlthau's Information Search Process (Kuhlthau 2004) is a foundational framework for information seeking in the library that includes a progression through:

- Initiation: When a person first becomes aware of a lack of knowledge or understanding, and feelings of uncertainty and apprehension are common;

- Selection: When a general area, topic, or problem is identified and initial uncertainty often gives way to a brief sense of optimism and a readiness to begin the search;

- Exploration: When inconsistent, incompatible information is encountered and uncertainty, confusion, and doubt frequently increase and people find their confidence flagging;

- Formulation: When a focused perspective is formed and uncertainty diminishes as confidence begins to increase;

- Collection: When information pertinent to the focused perspective is gathered and uncertainty subsides as interest and involvement deepens; and

- Presentation: When the search is completed with a new understanding enabling the person to explain his or her learning to others or in some way put the learning to use.

Similarly, the NGSS (Achieve, Inc. 2013) explicates eight science and engineering practices that are essential for all students to learn:

- Asking questions (for science) and defining problems (for engineering);
- Developing and using models;
- Planning and conducting investigations;
- Analyzing and interpreting data;
- Using mathematics and computational thinking;
- Constructing explanations (for science) and designing solutions (for engineering);
- Engaging in argument from evidence; and
- Obtaining, evaluating, and communicating information.

Both frameworks begin with identifying an information need and conclude with an opportunity for self-assessment and reflection.

Although objections to the NGSS have not reached the extent of the criticism engendered by the CCSS, the NGSS has elicited some concerns. Opponents contend that the science standards are vague, they stress scientific practices too much and should cover more theory, and that some states already have standards that are superior to the NGSS. Most notably, the Thomas B. Fordham Institute, producers of the *State of the Standards* reports, gave the NGSS a "C" grade, because the standards lacked essential content, such as the topic of covalent bonding in high school chemistry; overemphasized engineering practices, such as coming up with problems and models to solve them; and failed to integrate sufficient mathematics into science learning (Gross et al. 2013).

Other critics have expressed concern that basic content knowledge is needed before students can understand scientific and engineering practices, or how scientists "do science." Coupled with the lack of clarity specifically in what is expected from teachers, critics are concerned that the standards stress too many things at once and have the potential to overwhelm students (Asif 2013).

Learning Environments
for the Common Standards

Because they reflect a shift in instructional practice and a focus on inter-disciplinary connections and applications, the CCSS and NGSS thrive in learning environments that are student-centered, immersive, and provide intuitive access to an adequate quantity and comprehensive range of academically rigorous and relevant learning resources. As Figure 3.4 depicts, there are some learning environments particularly well suited to the learning tasks of the NGSS and CCSS.

As Figure 3.4 shows, optimal learning environments for the common standards include several key components. The common standards are based on the notion of building not just personal mastery, but personal relevance for the standards. The personalized learning environment requires interplay between the learner, the teacher's role, the learning environment, and the learning approaches employed. The learner should be in an environment that supports metacognition through discussion and individual contemplation regarding what information or topics should be considered, understood, or researched. Students should have a sense of why the learning activity is occurring. Likewise, an environment conducive to the common standards supports self-actualization. Students require the opportunity to reflect and realize the extent to which their own problem-solving abilities are growing as a result of newly acquired knowledge and experiences. Figure 3.5 gives an overview of the shift in instructional effort.

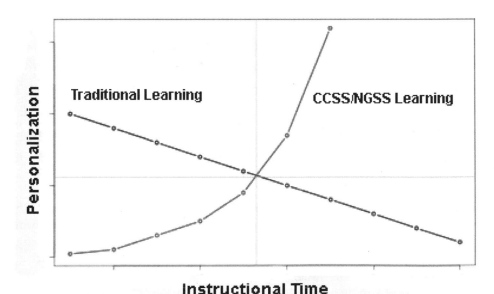

Figure 3.4. Elements of an optimal CCSS/NGSS learning environment.

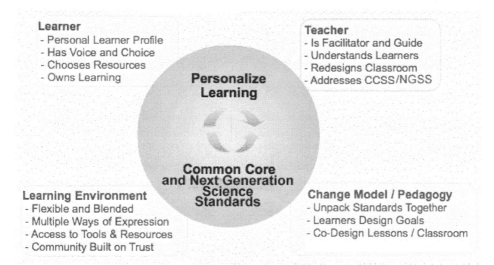

Figure 3.5. Personalization and instructional time in common standards–based and traditional learning.

As Figure 3.5 shows, the object of a shift to a common standards–based learning environment is to increase the amount of time students engage in personalized learning and decrease the amount of time teachers spend on traditional explicit instruction. When knowledge is both constructed and deconstructed in the course of a learning activity, students are able to enhance and express the abilities that result from newly acquired knowledge and experiences that displace prior knowledge and experiences.

Contextual or application competencies and their associated instructional shifts provide great entry points for librarians. The introduction of the English/language arts standards document sets the scene for librarians' involvement by stating that students who meet the standards

> habitually perform the critical reading necessary to pick carefully through the staggering amount of information available today in print and digitally. They actively seek the wide, deep, and thoughtful engagement with high-quality literary and informational texts that builds knowledge, enlarges experience, and broadens worldviews. They reflexively demonstrate the cogent reasoning and use of evidence that is essential to both private deliberation and responsible citizenship in a democratic republic. (Common Core State Standards Initiative 2010, 3)

The CCSS authors go on to state that the ELA standards have information and media skills woven throughout—just the type of contextual learning promoted by the AASL *Standards for the 21st Century Learner* (AASL 2009b). The crosswalks and standards associations in the NGSS make it easy for teachers and librarians to see links to information skills in Practices and Crosscutting Concepts. The CCSS and NGSS give teachers and learners a framework in which to place information; information can help learners see that literacy is a matter not just of *how*, but also of *why*.

Conclusion

The widespread adoption of the NGSS and CCSS represents a rare alignment of the legislative, pedagogical, and technology trends currently impacting education. This provides an opportunity to dramatically and positively evolve K–12 education. Pressures to adopt digital tests, cut instructional materials costs, and comply with accountability and reporting requirements might compel K–12 leaders to quickly embrace proprietary solutions to meet the NGSS and CCSS. As Escambia County (Florida) Chief Technology Officer Don Manderson pointed out, "Putting in place a next generation, interoperable digital learning ecosystem is key to positively impacting the core competency of K–12 by empowering teachers to be more efficient and effective in delivering . . . personalized instruction" (Manderson 2012, 8).

The key item to know about commons standards is that they focus on competency. Yet standards often end up in the background, mostly ignored because teachers must prepare students to excel on tests and also to protect teachers' high-stakes evaluations. Textbook publishers could make the most superficial changes and assert that their instructional materials are "aligned" with the standards. Teacher preparation programs might simply ignore them. But it doesn't have to be this way. As researchers from Fordham pointed out,

> Standards are the foundation upon which almost everything else rests—or should rest. They should guide state assessments and accountability systems; inform teacher preparation, licensure, and professional development; and give shape to curricula, textbooks, software programs, and more. Choose your metaphor: Standards are targets, or blueprints, or roadmaps. They set the destination: what we want our students to know and be able to do by the end of their K–12 experience, and the benchmarks they should reach along the way. If the standards are vague, watered-down, or misguided, they can point our schools down perilous paths. If there are no standards worth following, there is no education destination worth reaching. (Finn, Petrilli, and Julian 2006, 10)

Taking It Further: Professional Development Resources

Achieve, Inc. and American Association of School Librarians. 2013. "Implementing the Common Core State Standards: The Role of the School Librarian." *Action Brief.* Accessed September 8, 2014. http://www.achieve.org/files/CCSSLibrariansBrief-FINAL.pdf.

American Association of School Librarians. 2014. "Learning Standards & Common Core State Standards Crosswalk." http://www.ala.org/aasl/standards-guidelines/crosswalk.

The Hunt Institute. 2012. *Common Core Implementation,* Video Series. http://www.youtube.com/user/TheHuntInstitute#g/u.

CHAPTER 4

Curation Part 1

Selecting and Describing STEM Digital Resources

Chapter Highlights

- The current state of STEM collections

- Digital resources and collection development

- Getting started: Assessing needs

- Choosing quality STEM resources

- Describing STEM resources

Introduction

As discussed in the previous chapters, K–12 STEM teaching and
learning have changed. Whereas teachers once were left to their own
devices (and the aid of their school librarians) to identify and integrate
high-quality learning resources, the recent federal educational initiatives
have transformed instructional materials selection from one based on
"pull" (i.e., resources gained from colleagues, search engines, specialized digital libraries) to one based on "push" (i.e., resources presented
to teachers in the context of standards- and assessment-linked student
data systems or a digital library). This fundamental change in the way
teachers create their instructional plans stems from the curriculum standards movement and the drive to personalize learning.

Thus far, this book has looked at what constitutes STEM learning, and how good STEM learning and teaching are closely linked to best practices in school librarianship. It then examined the common standards movement and the shifts in educator and student activity to conceptual understanding and application. STEM learning that is driven by common standards rests on quality learning resources that enable personalization. This chapter explores the role digital resources, especially open educational resources (OER), created for K–12 STEM.

The Current State of STEM Collections

More teachers are "out of field" in science than in any other area of K–12 education (Ellis 2013; National Council on Teacher Quality 2014). Perhaps this lack of experience with science topics combined with the importance of science achievement accounts for many teachers' reliance on science textbooks (Fang 2014; Roseman, Stern, and Koppal 2010; Ulerick [n.d.]). Stern and Roseman (2004) reviewed middle school science textbooks, however, and found that the leading textbook series rarely present important ideas in ways that challenge students to construct knowledge and gain deep topical understanding. Some material conveyed through textbooks thus might counter the goals of inquiry-based, constructivist learning advocated by the CCSS, NGSS, and related federal initiatives (Trygstad et al. 2013). Textbook materials also lack elements for engaging reluctant students in linking science and mathematics to real-world problems (Shapiro 2012). STEM collections also tend to be problematic for school librarians.

Although STEM is the disciplinary area for which most digital resources have been created (American Association of School Librarians [AASL] 2011; Boston Consulting Group 2013; Project Tomorrow 2012b; School Library Journal 2013), studies have suggested that STEM teachers lack the time and skill to locate and integrate new instructional materials without assistance (Kay 2012; Kay and Knaack 2009a, 2009b). The shift to digital learning resources, especially OER, in STEM still appears to be unstoppable (Porcello and Hsi 2013) and, as discussed in Chapter 2, many STEM teachers do not perceive their school librarians as sources of help because they perceive school collections to be old and small (Mardis 2004). Indeed, STEM collections often prove to be out of date and small in relation to other curriculum areas (Mardis and Hoffman 2007a). However, STEM teachers are the largest group using digital resources, especially OER, as Figure 4.1 shows.

As Figure 4.1 suggests, STEM teachers, even with little the time and expertise to select high-quality resources, are using great quantities

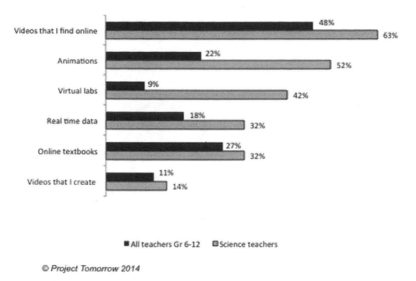

Figure 4.1. Teachers' use of digital resources (Project Tomorrow 2014).

of videos, animations, data sets, virtual labs, and online textbooks. Although instructional partnering of STEM teachers with their school librarians seems unlikely and use of the STEM collection is rare, school librarians who can promote well-curated collections of digital resources can provide a vital service to their learning community.

School Librarians as Collection Developers and Curators

School librarians lead in the context of very specialized libraries in which collections are curated to reflect the curriculum mandates, community norms, learning extension, and personal enrichment of the school's very specific population. The deep involvement of a variety of stakeholders including students, teachers, administrators, and parents ensures that the collection meets these needs and that shifting values and needs are reflected in library materials (Mardis et al. 2012). Many school librarians struggle with science collection development because they lack formal education in this area (Young 2001). Science information changes very quickly, and information in recently published books often is outdated before the books are placed on the library shelves. In many instances, STEM information older than seven years is considered out of date. Staying abreast of developments in scientific fields to maintain a current science collection can be the most challenging collection development task a school librarian faces.

Because digital resources are a growing part of educators' learning resource base (Collins and Levy 2013; Mickey and Meaney 2010, 2011; Simba Information 2014), open educational resources are a key element of twenty-first century school library collections (Digital Textbook Collaborative 2012; Mardis and Everhart 2013; Mickey and Meaney 2013). Digital learning materials such as lesson plans, videos of instructional practice, and formative assessments can improve the classroom experience for all students, and they could hold particular promise for students with disabilities. OER often are designed and developed with flexibility and customization capabilities at the outset—reflecting the principles of universal design—and can be revised in a more timely manner than the labor-intensive and costly process of updating traditional, static materials like printed textbooks. Digital content can be designed, created, and refined over time in a way that recognizes and responds to the full spectrum of learner variability. These tools and resources can be integrated into library collections to meet individual student needs. Access to repositories of high-quality content has been listed as a national priority (SETDA and Education Counsel LLC 2014).

Due to the sheer quantity of OER available, curation is crucial to ensure that evolving definitions of quality are reflected in the collection (Rosenbaum 2011). Some in the educational community cite the "great piles of stuff" that are composed of accessible learning resources which

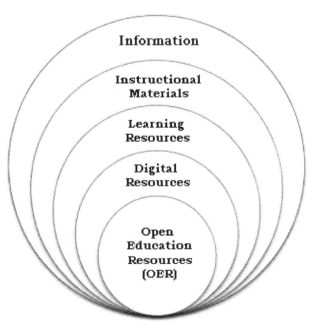

Figure 4.2. Types of materials in school library collections.

should be transformed into "piles of great stuff" (Zia 2005, para. 1) that is current, content rich, authoritative, and effective in communicating learning concepts. This notion of not just collecting the resources, but of actively seeking them out in response to curriculum needs, stakeholder priorities, and learning personalization concerns, puts school librarians in the dynamic role of curator. Resources must be described and organized in ways that maximize access (SETDA and Education Counsel LLC 2014). Figure 4.2 shows the placement of OER in the context of the larger body of materials that school librarians traditionally curate.

Although the benefits of using open educational resources versus costly commercial instructional materials are evident, problems of determining OER quality have persisted for more than two decades (Hanson and Carlson 2005; Mardis 2003; Mardis and Howe 2010; Mardis and Zia 2003). In an unpublished report of a 2013 meeting of statewide education officials hosted by the National Science Digital Library (NSDL), participants stated a dependence on—and a fear of losing—an adequate supply of high-quality STEM OER. State education policymakers cited forces such as a lack of curation strategies to manage collections; insufficient resources to identify and vet OER; and a strong desire to automate the selection, validation, and management processes as essential issues to resolve if their transitions to delivering CCSS- and NGSS-based curriculum were to be successful (Hewlett Foundation 2013; Okerson 2000).

Getting Started

Collection development is the foundation upon which curation rests. To this end, a strong plan for a STEM collection is essential for STEM curation. Experts in collection development agree that the process of building a collection is best begun with an awareness of the learning community and a needs assessment of key stakeholders (Bishop 2013; Evans 2012; Pattee 2014). In the context of STEM, understanding curriculum targets, types of learning activities, and teachers' and students' preferences for topics and resource types are key determinations. For digital resources, it also is important to discern computer and projector availability and bandwidth capacity.

After the library users' needs have been established, librarians should critically examine their existing resource base. Free, automated, collection-analysis tools such as Follett School Solution's *TitleWise*[1] and Mackin Education Resources' *Collection Analysis Plus Solutions* (CAPS)[2] can quickly and easily help librarians determine the ages and extent of their collections in STEM areas. STEM areas usually include Dewey Decimal Classification ranges for 000 (Generalities), 500

Age Sensitivity

Dewey Ranges	Acceptable Age (Years)	Items in Collection	Aged	
003-007 Systems Data/Computer Programs	3	4	3	75.00%
320-329 Political Science	5	21	11	52.38%
361-369 Social Problems and Services	5	44	28	63.64%
370-379 Education	5	22	18	81.82%
380-389 Commerce, Communications and Transportation	5	47	39	82.98%
520-529 Astronomy and Allied Sciences	5	118	83	70.34%
570-579 Life Sciences/Biology	5	75	45	60.00%
610-619 Medical Sciences/Medicine	5	119	74	62.18%
910-919 Geography, Maps, Atlases	5	136	127	93.38%

Figure 4.3. Same age analysis from Follett's TitleWise tool.

(Natural Science and Mathematics), and 600 (Technology and Medicine). As Figure 4.3 shows, these tools also provide reports that include target average copyright dates.

Curriculum maps also can inform collection maps. As STEM teachers look to ensure congruence between classroom activities and the NGSS and CCSS, they map those activities to the standards. School librarians can match those standards and teachers' current instructional materials to resources in their collection to identify strengths and gaps.

Locating Open Educational Resources

Traditional instructional materials primarily are reviewed for content accuracy, particularly in the STEM fields (Campbell and Barker 2013). As materials have become more digital and state and national curriculum standards increasingly influential, these media-quality and standards alignment issues also have become routinely considered (Spiegel 1989; and Roseman 2004). In an autonomous search mode, when teachers assess quality "on the fly," sentiment and quality determination tend to vary widely from teacher to teacher and resource to resource (Hanson and Carlson 2005; Mardis et al. 2012), with some teachers favoring assessments based on appearance and some favoring assessments based on content (Perrault 2007; Recker et al. 2011; Recker et al. 2007). For this reason, many teachers and education policymakers have expressed preferences for repositories of vetted resources with clear designations of quality, utility, and curriculum support (Price 2007).

Armed with an evidence-based and prioritized list for collection revitalization, school librarians must begin identifying resources. As discussed previously in this chapter, although appropriate resources can be identified through Web searches or found in a number of fee-based commercial sources such as netTrekker and WebPathExpress, educators and policymakers are increasingly seeing OER as an important source of learning content. Starting points for metadata (descriptive records) for high quality K–12 STEM OER include educational digital libraries such as those listed below.

National Science Digital Library (http://nsdl.org)

 Far more than a repository of online STEM OER, the National Science Digital Library (NSDL) (http://nsdl.org) is a networked source of 127 education-focused collections. The National Science Foundation (NSF) established the NSDL program in 2000 as an online library of exemplary digital resources for STEM education and research at all educational levels. The collection is searchable and also is browsable in a number of ways that enable access to the right resource. Highlights for the school library collection include the following.

- The 18 NSDL **Pathways** are discipline-specific (biology, chemistry, climate science and literacy, computational science, computing sciences, Earth sciences, engineering, materials science, mathematics, physics and astronomy, social sciences/quantitative literacy) and education level-specific partnerships (middle school, K–12 multimedia, community and technical colleges, informal education) that provide stewardship for the educational content and services needed by major communities of learners.

- The NSDL **Common Core Math Collection** provides easy access to high-quality math resources that have been related to one or more CCSS mathematics standards. These 388 resources (to date) are selected from the NSDL collection and trusted providers, and are organized by grade level and domain area. Resource types can include assessment material, answer keys, rubrics, tests, data sets, instructional materials, activities, demonstrations, games, instructor guides or manuals, lesson plans, problem sets, instructional units, numerical models, and more. To directly access the collection, visit http://nsdl.org/browse/commcore/math/.

- **Science Refreshers** service (http://nsdl.org/refreshers) supports elementary educators with resources selected from among NSDL collections that are best suited to help teachers brush up on their science content knowledge as they are preparing their classroom lessons.

- The NSDL **Science Literacy Maps** (http://strandmaps.nsdl.org) help K–12 teachers find NSDL resources that relate to specific science and math concepts, and reinforce their own conceptual frameworks. These maps, based on the American Association for the Advancement of Science (AAAS) Project 2061's *Atlas of Science Literacy*, illustrate connections between concepts as well as how concepts build upon one another across grade levels.

- NSDL on **iTunes U** offers multimedia resources for science and math education, including videos, podcasts, and educator guides that can help to augment content knowledge as well as be incorporated into classroom use.

During the last 15 years, the NSDL has witnessed and collectively adapted to a variety of educational trends and sea changes—in technology use; social practice; technological and pedagogical content knowledge acquisition and expertise; adaptations of technology to educator professional development; understanding of the way people learn; and evolving expertise about digital learning (McIlvain 2010). Use of the NSDL website and related search and reference services is free, as are the majority of the resources discoverable through NSDL. Use of the NSDL site does not require creating an account. As of October 1, 2014, NSDI became a collection in the stewardship of OER Commons. It is antiicipated that NSDL will continue to occupy its role as a leading STEM content provider.

OER Commons (http://www.oercommons.org)

Founded early in 2008 by the Institute for Knowledge Management in Education (ISKME) with support from the Hewlett Foundation, OER Commons is a free teaching and learning network that contains a digital library of more than 30,000 vetted educational resources in all K–12 and undergraduate curriculum areas and professional development materials. Resources on the site can be searched and filtered, and contain descriptions that reflect usage rights and standards alignments in addition to standard descriptive information. Users can tag, rate, review, and share materials. Figure 4.4 features a typical display for an OER Commons resource.

The OER Commons includes metadata for over 55,000 resources from collections such as Khan Academy,[3] the Nobel Foundation,[4] and TEDed.[5] The OER Commons can be searched, browsed by topic, and browsed by special collection. It also provides professional development, standards alignment, personal curation, and authoring tools that allow users to integrate Web 2.0 technologies to enhance their OER use

Figure 4.4. Record for an OER Commons resource.

skills and make best use of the content. Those tools and special features include the following.

- **Open Author** lets users combine text, pictures, sound, files and video. Saved as openly licensed educational resources, users/authors can share their combinations with friends, colleagues, and educators around the world.

- The **Common Core Alignment and OER Evaluation Tool** is found on all Resource Pages in OER Commons. This tool can be used to quickly and easily align appropriate resources to the Common Core State Standards, and to evaluate the resource against certain aspects of quality.

- **Learner Options.** A particular strength of the OER Commons is its commitment to accessibility. The "Learner Options" feature on each page of the website enables users to change display of the site to meet a range of viewing preferences.

- **Use Guidelines** for each resource are labeled with one of four conditions. These at-a-glance labels can help users quickly distinguish whether a resource can be changed or shared without further permission required. It also provides the specific license or terms of permitted use for each resource.

- **Bookmark Tool** allows users to easily recommend educational resources from the Internet to the OER Commons. Users need only drag the Bookmark Button from the OER Commons Contribute page to their browser's "Favorites" toolbar.

The OER Commons is a dynamic collection that adds new features all the time. Recent focuses include resources that support collections of social and emotional learning, flexible learning, and game-based learning.

Selecting Resources

By starting with vetted resources from digital libraries such as NSDL and OER Commons, librarians can shift their collection efforts from location and initial quality considerations to subtler, locally tailored resource features.

Quality

Most quality considerations for OER are the same as those recommended by major collection development texts such as Kay Bishop's *Collection Program in Schools* (2013). As Table 4.1 reflects, other organizations have created quality checklists for OER. In 2001, the Council on Library and Information Resources (CLIR) introduced *Building Sustainable Collections of Free Third-Party Web Resources* (Pitschmann 2001). In 2011, education reform organization and common standards co-sponsor Achieve created an OER rubric that can be used independently or through the resource evaluation tool built into OER Commons (Achieve, Inc. 2011). Finally, in 2012, the NSDL created the Resource Quality Checklist to provide guidance for reviewing and selecting resources for inclusion in their collections (NSDL 2012).

Table 4.1. Comparison of Selection Criteria

CLIR	Bishop	Achieve	NSDL
Context			
Provenance			X
Relationship to Other Resources	X		X
Content			
Validity	X	X	X
Accuracy	X	X	X
Authority	X	X	X
Uniqueness	X		X
Completeness	X	X	X
Coverage	X	X	
Currency			X
Audience	X	X	X
Accessibility			
Composition and Site Organization	X	X	X
Navigational Features	X	X	X
Adheres to Recognizes Access Standards		X	X
User Support Content		X	X
Terms, Conditions, and Rights Statements		X	X
Process or Technical			
Information Integrity			X
Site Integrity			X
System Integrity			X
Additional criteria: • Aligned to Standards (Achieve, NSDL) • Engaging for Learners (Achieve, NSDL) • Feedback Features/Feedback Available (NSDL) • Opportunities for Deeper Learning (Achieve) • Reusable and Adaptable (NSDL)			

As Table 4.1 demonstrates, resource quality centers on considerations context, content, and accessibility. Context applies to the relation of the resource to other items in the collection, or its granularity. This aspect is discussed in depth below. Content considerations relate to the validity, accuracy, authority, uniqueness, completeness, coverage, currency, and audience of a resource. These considerations ensure that the resource is appropriate for the community and collection areas identified in the needs assessment. Accessibility and technical considerations relate to the implementation of the resource: Sites that host OERs must be easy to organize, have terms and conditions that permit the intended uses, and be accessible to learners with special considerations such as diverse language and physical access needs.

Additional considerations common to one or more of the criteria checklists include contemporary considerations such as standards alignment, learner engagement, ability to view and contribute ratings and reviews, support for deep learning, and reusability.

Granularity

As defined in the introduction, granularity refers to the size of the resource. Librarians should be comfortable with the notion of granularity because, as shown in Figure 4.5, it is a concept much like the notational hierarchy of the Dewey Decimal Classification System.

The challenge for librarians is to match their collection development practices to the level of granularity that best serves the learning task. If a student has a question about the biomes of a specific location, for example, it might not be appropriate to point the student to a collection of OER that relates to biomes; instead, the student would benefit from a resource about biomes in the target region. School librarians might find multiple levels of granularity appropriate for their collection needs.

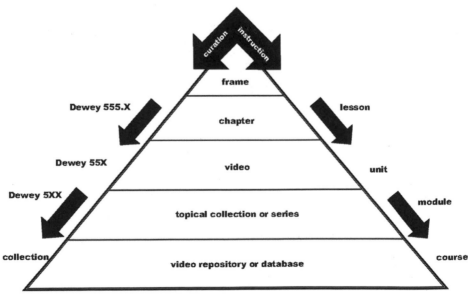

Figure 4.5. OER granularity levels for curation and instruction.

Resource Type

Moreover, the growing array of resource types demands expertise not only in identifying high-quality or trustworthy resources; curating also means recommending the right resource in both content and format. The levels of discernment required by curators are unprecedented and lead to niche expertise tailored to a particular information market and the needs of a unique audience (Rosenbaum 2011).

School librarians can aid learning personalization by matching students with resource types appropriate for their needs. Resource types provide a useful starting point for thinking about the range of OER available. Relevant OER could be in the form of animations; assessments; audio files; ebooks; ebook chapters; data sets; games; learning modules; reference materials; texts; tutorials; simulations; worksheets; and video files (Shank 2014). Note that this list includes items at varying levels of granularity; the resource type and level of granularity must be considered in relation to the learning task. Figure 4.6 provides an overview of some possible combinations of these factors organized by Bloom's taxonomy of learning complexity.

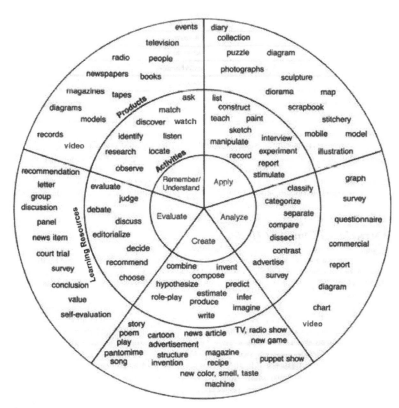

Figure 4.6. Bloom's Taxonomy mapped to activities, products, and learning resources.

Each segment of the interior circle is important, but certainly "remember" and "create" involves different levels of learner investment. Each of these activities requires different kinds of support in the collection. The collection undoubtedly will favor some resource types over others. As Figure 4.1 suggests, STEM teachers enthusiastically use digital video. This contention is supported by a number of studies: Kirschenbaum (2006) found that contemporary students learned better through highly visual presentation, and other researchers have suggested that multimodal learning helped to activate essential prior knowledge, the platform upon which subsequent learning takes place (Bransford, Brown, and Cocking 2000; Hirsch 2006; Roschelle 1995). Access to video delivered in a variety of formats also was shown to be a very important aspect of school librarians' service to STEM educators (Mardis 2009), and school library video collections also appeared to have a strong role in student STEM achievement (Mardis 2007). Many OER repository collections (e.g., OER Commons, Khan Academy, and PBS LearningMedia) have substantial video collections; a comprehensive list of free online collections of STEM digital video is listed in Appendix B.

Rights

Open educational resources might not be fee-based, but that does not mean that they can be used without any consideration of attribution and reuse restrictions. Tools such as the OER Commons authoring tool enable users to combine OER into new and personalized resources, but these new combinations might not always respect the use conditions of the individual resources. As a result, many collection providers include rights information about their OER. As Table 4.2 shows, for example, rights statements from OER Commons and PBS Learning Media reflect a range of restriction levels.

As students become information creators as well as information consumers, ensuring that available resources are used appropriately is an aspect of the school librarian's role that will remain important and likely will gain prominence.

Describing Resources

Integrating OER into a physical collection poses particular challenges for description. Librarians customarily catalog items with a definite beginning and end, such as books, DVDs, and journal articles. Many of these resources have tables of contents, indexes, or abstracts that can inform the descriptive record. Many others have records that can be purchased from publishers or downloaded from other catalogers.

Table 4.2. OER Commons and PBS LearningMedia OER Rights Statements

OER Commons	PBS LearningMedia
No Strings Attached – No restrictions on remixing, redistributing, or making derivative works. Give credit to the author, as required.	**Stream, Download, Share, and Modify** — Users are permitted to download, edit, distribute, and make derivative works of the content. Users must attribute the content as indicated in the attribution file.
Remix and Share – Remixing, redistributing, or making derivative works comes with some restrictions, including how it is shared.	**Stream, Download, and Share** — Users are permitted to download the content, make verbatim copies of the content, incorporate the content unmodified into a presentation (such as an essay or Web page), and distribute verbatim copies of the content, but you may not edit or alter the content or create any derivative works of the content. Users must attribute the content as indicated in the attribution file.
Share Only – Redistribution comes with some restrictions. Do not remix or make derivative works.	**Stream and Download** — Users are permitted to download the content to view it on a computer or other digital video device for their own personal use. Users may not modify, redistribute, reproduce, edit, retransmit, or in any way repurpose the content. Use of the content must conform to restrictions indicated in the associated attribution file.
Read the Fine Print – All Rights Reserved. U.S.-based educators have certain permissions under Fair Use and the TEACH Act that include educational and personal uses of copyrighted materials, custom licenses and terms, permission to print only, unknown restrictions, and any other redistribution restrictions.	**Stream Only** — Users are permitted only to stream the content from the site. Users may save links to the content in their PBS LearningMedia accounts and may also incorporate html links to the URLs of the Resource Pages for this content. They are not permitted to download this content.

Also, users understand that if a book is a textbook about a course, then they will have to search the book for a chapter on a particular topic. For OER, the resource is not a physical entity and it can be difficult to define a discrete beginning and end, and harder to accommodate for various uses.

This situation makes it a challenge to determine exactly what constitutes the digital resource to be cataloged (granularity). For instance, if an engineering course module that has applets and animations about dynamite that can be used in several contexts, then the librarian must decide whether to catalog the course as a whole and then make separate catalog entries for the applets and animations, or choose some other descriptive strategy.

To solve this dilemma, librarians might wish to first catalog the enveloping resource for its intended use. Regardless of whether a librarian loves to catalog or hates it, chances are very good that the librarian either buys machine readable catalog (MARC) records; "copy catalogs" the MARC records by downloading them from another source; or creates MARC records from scratch.

For units or graphics within a resource, librarians can create additional metadata records tailored to reflect the various educational, technical, or pedagogical applications of the granular item. So for the example given above, the librarian first would create a metadata record to describe the course, and then catalog the individual applets and animations, relate them, and note these relationships within the related records (Ginger 2012). This approach reflects the best practices for determining a cataloging approach as recommended by the Digital Library for Earth Systems Education (DLESE).[6]

- Generally create a single metadata record for resources as a whole. Create additional metadata records for a whole resource if individual parts of a resource differ substantially in technical requirements, descriptions, and educational information.

- Create relationships between resources using the fields of relation and occasionally, learning resource type and description. Be careful in using description and learning resource type so as not to give information that should be cataloged in a second metadata record.

- Apply the relationship concept described above to strike a balance between supporting resource discovery with reasonable user effort and to avoid potential user frustration with retrieving many redundant records.

- Recognize that community-developed collections can have varying levels of granularity (Ginger 2012).

Although this process might seem laborious, solutions are on the horizon that should make it easier to create and share records for both physical and digital resources (*see* Box 4.1). While the professional fully transitions to RDA and BIBFRAME, a few other options for importing and creating descriptive records for the OPAC/library management system are available.

Cataloging can be one of the most hated tasks a librarian undertakes. The process of understanding a work and determining how to describe it for others in a way that is not only consistent, but also intellectually accessible, however, is important. After all, as librarians, aren't we responsible for helping our clients find information in ways that are empowering and translate to other contexts? This book looks at ways to integrate OER records into an existing MARC-based online public access catalog (OPAC) or library management system (LMS) such as Follett School Solutions' Destiny Library Manager[7] or COMPanion's Alexandria.[8]

Box 4.1. Resource Description and Access (RDA) and BIBFRAME: A Solution for Integrated Collections

The American Library Association, Canadian Library Association, and Chartered Institute of Library and Information Professionals (CILIP) launched *RDA: Resource Description and Access* as the new standard for resource description and access designed for the digital world. Built on the foundations established by the *Anglo-American Cataloguing Rules, Second Edition* (AACR2), RDA provides a comprehensive set of guidelines and instructions on resource description and access covering all types of content and media. Benefits of RDA include:

- A structure based on the conceptual models of functional requirements for bibliographic data (FRBR) and functional requirements for authority data (FRAD) to help catalog users find the information they need more easily;

- A flexible framework for content description of digital resources that also serves the needs of libraries organizing traditional resources; and

- A better fit with emerging database technologies, enabling institutions to introduce efficiencies in data capture and storage retrievals.

The Library of Congress' BIBFRAME Initiative is a foundation for the future of bibliographic description that happens on the Web and in the networked world. It is designed to integrate with and engage in the wider information community and still serve the very specific needs of libraries. The BIBFRAME Initiative brings new ways to:

- Differentiate clearly between conceptual content and its physical/digital manifestation(s);

- Unambiguously identify information entities (e.g., authorities); and

- Leverage and expose relationships between and among entities.

In a Web-scale world, it is imperative to be able to cite library data in a way that differentiates the conceptual work (i.e., a title and author) from the physical details about that work's manifestation (e.g., page numbers, whether it has illustrations). It is equally important to produce library data so that it clearly identifies entities involved in the creation of a resource (authors, publishers) and the concepts (subjects) associated with a resource.

Find out more at: http://www.rdatoolkit.org/ and http://www.loc.gov/bibframe/.

Import OER Records

Getting metadata from OER providers into a library collection can be done in a number of ways. NSDL allows the XML for individual collections to be downloaded through its OAI Data Provider Tool.[9] A list of NSDL collections, number of records per collection, and a description of each collection with records available for download is located in Appendix B. The records are exported in XML format.

Folletts' Destiny system allows for the import of XML records. Many resources are available to walk users through that process, and Section 4.10 (Taking It Further) of this chapter includes pointers to a few helpful sources for directions and support. Librarians also can convert XML to MARC using free and open source tools such a MARCEdit (see link in Section 4.10, Taking It Further, below).

Create OER Records

Of course, librarians always can create MARC records from scratch. Help is available for those who are not comfortable cataloging.Web-2MARC is a tool especially created to help school librarians quickly and easily create catalog records for any URL in four easy steps, as shown in Figure 4.7.

In Step 0, users locate an object to catalog. In this example case, we are cataloging a video from PBS LearningMedia. Highlight and copy the URL in the Web browser bar.

In Step 1, users paste the URL into the Web2MARC address box at http://dl2sl.org/web2marc. Web2MARC already has a large selection of records from NSDL and other providers that a user can browse and download by Dewey class or keyword search.

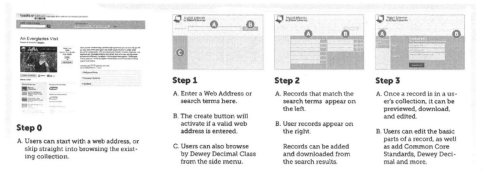

Figure 4.7. Web2MARC process overview.

Step 0

A. Users can start with a web address, or skip straight into browsing the existing collection.

Step 1

A. Enter a Web Address or search terms here.

B. The create button will activate if a valid web address is entered.

C. Users can also browse by Dewey Decimal Class from the side menu.

Step 2

A. Records that match the search terms appear on the left.

B. User records appear on the right.

Records can be added and downloaded from the search results.

Step 3

A. Once a record is in a user's collection, it can be previewed, download, and edited.

B. Users can edit the basic parts of a record, as well as add Common Core Standards, Dewey Decimal and more.

In Step 2, users can download a displayed record or click "Create Record" at the end of the Web2MARC address box. If a record for the URL already exists in Web2MARC, then it is displayed. If the record does not already exist, then Web2MARC, behind the scenes, visits the URL and populates a new MARC record with information found on that site. That information typically includes title, author, description, and keywords.

In Step 3, users can edit the MARC record to meet their local needs. Editing considerations include the following.

Controlled Vocabulary

Web2MARC has Library of Congress Subject Headings (LCSH)[10] and auto-completes a typed word to match the closest LCSH term.

Uncontrolled Vocabulary

This field can include keywords of the users' choosing. Popular keywords include adjectives like "scary," teachers' names (e.g., "Mrs. Kinkaid), grade level (e.g., grade 3), or video run time (e.g., 3:50). If the resource requires a login, this field also is the place to note that information. Use this field to ensure that library users can quickly locate records to meet their needs.

Standards Assignment

Web2MARC includes two standards assignment tools: the CCSS tool that allows users to keyword search or browse the ELA and mathematics standards and add them to a record. In late 2014, Web2MARC debuted an NGSS assignment tool that helps users link resources to those standards. Web2MARC automatically places the standards codes in the correct MARC field so that a user can see them in the catalog record.

Note that this field is not called "standards alignment." Standards alignment is a process in which a resource is deemed to be effective to teach and learn the concepts reflected within a standard. To be aligned, the content addressed in OER must match the content addressed in the proposed standard. Evaluating the alignment of the performances required in both the object and the standard is equally essential and should be considered along with the content. Content-area teachers might wish to provide feedback about whether a resource that is assigned a standard also is aligned to that standard (Achieve, Inc. 2011).

Any MARC record can be tailored using these considerations. Tools such as Web2MARC can make record creation quick and easy, however, to enable librarians to focus on making it accessible to library users. After the record has been edited to reflect the school community's needs, Web2MARC users can either save the record to their free account or download the record for immediate import into the library OPAC.

Notes

1. Follett School Solutions. *TitleWise.* http://www.titlewave.com/intro/titleservices.html.
2. Mackin Education Resources. *Collection Analysis Plus Solutions* (CAPS). http://www.mackin.com/COLLECTIONMGMT/MAIN.aspx.
3. Khan Academy. https://www.khanacademy.org/.
4. The Nobel Foundation. http://www.nobelprize.org/educational/.
5. TEDed. http://ed.ted.com/.
6. Digital Library for Earth Systems Education (DLESE). http://dlese.org.
7. Follett School Solutions. Destiny Library Manager. http://www.follettsoftware.com/library-automation-software.
8. COMPanion. Alexandria. http://www.goalexandria.com/.
9. NSDL. OAI Data Provider Tool. http://nsdl.org/nsdl_dds/services/oaiDataProvider/oai_explorer.jsp.
10. Library of Congress Subject Headings (LCSH). http://www.loc.gov/catdir/cpso/lcco/.

Taking It Further: Tips and Tools

More About OER

- Connexions online course about working with OER is available at http://cnx.org/content/m15211/latest/.

- The UNESCO *OER Toolkit* is available at http://oerwiki.iiep-unesco .org /index.php?title=UNESCO_OER_Toolkit.

- WikiEducator *OER Handbook for Educators* is available at http://wikieducator.org /OER_Handbook/educator_version_one/ Introduction/Why_OER%3F.

More About Cataloging

Campbell, D. G. 2000. "Straining the Standards: How Cataloging Web Sites for Curriculum Support Poses Fresh Problems for the Anglo American Cataloging Rules." *Journal of Internet Cataloging* 3 (1): 79–92.

Follett. *Overview of Destiny's XML Upload Capability.* http://legacy-help.fsc.follett.com /Content/textbooks/classes/xml_upload_ overview.htm.

Fountain, J. F., J. E. Gilchrist, and S. S. Intner (eds.). 2011. *Cataloging Correctly for Kids: An Introduction to the Tools,* 5th ed. Chicago, IL: American Library Association.

Haynes, F. 2004. "Cataloging 101: How to Get the Most Out of Your Online Catalog. In *Educational Media and Technology Yearbook 2004,* edited by M. A. Fitzgerald, M. Orey, and R. M. Branch, 274–81. Santa Barbara, CA: Libraries Unlimited.

Hoffman, G. L. 2009. "Meeting Users' Needs in Cataloging: What's the Right Thing to Do?" *Cataloging and Classification Quarterly* 47 (7): 631–41. doi: 10.180/01639370090111999.

Kaplan, A. G. 2004. "Meta-What? Metadata and Information Management for School Library Media Collections." Paper presented at the 27th American Educational Communications and Technology [AECT] Conference, Chicago, IL, October 19–23, 2004.

Letarte, K. 2000. "The School Library Media Center in the Digital Age: Issues in the Cataloging of Electronic Resources." *Journal of Internet Cataloging* 3 (1): 13–40.

MARCEdit. This tool includes a very rich feature set targeted at making metadata translation and editing easier for both beginning and advanced users. The tool translates XML to MARC, enables editing of MARC records, and includes many other features. http://marcedit.reeset.net/.

Murphy, C. 1995. *Curriculum-Enhanced MARC: A New Cataloging Format for School Librarians*. Education Resources Information Center (ERIC) ED 399952.

Plummer, K. A. 2000. "Cataloging K–12 Math and Science Curriculum Resources on the Internet: A Nontraditional Approach." *Journal of Internet Cataloging* 3 (1): 53–65.

CHAPTER 5

Curation Part 2

Managing and Promoting Your STEM OER Collection

Chapter Highlights

- Link checking and weeding
- Promoting collections to
  - Students
  - Teachers
  - Parents and community
  - Administrators

Introduction

The curatorial enterprise is comprised of resource identification, selection, management, and promotion (Bethard et al. 2009; Porcello and Hsi 2013; Wetzler et al. 2013). The previous chapter looked at identifying and selecting open educational resources (OER) as well as ways to describe the resources and include them in an online catalog. Of course, there are numerous other ways to include OER in a library collection other than to include them in the online public access catalog (OPAC), but by thinking of the OPAC as a "one-stop shop" for information resources, it is easier to keep track of the collection and direct users to a single search (Aptaker 2013). This chapter focuses on the final two steps of OER curation: management and promotion.

Managing the OER Collection

Collection management is an ongoing task that is informed by two main factors: policy and data (Evans and Zarnosky Saponaro 2012).

Policy Considerations

As with a print collection, the goal and procedures should be included in the library policies. Figure 5.1 provides an overview of policy layers that can affect the school library collection.

For OER, school and district policies might be important because they tend to emphasize learning priorities and technology considerations. For example, the district and school policies could specifically emphasize a commitment to supporting multicultural learning and/or ensuring accessibility by all students. Likewise, a school or district technology policy might restrict the use of streaming video or promote the replacement of print instructional materials with their digital equivalents. These are principles that you should ensure are reflected in your collection development policy.

Library policies might govern how library resources can be accessed after hours or beyond the school's walls. School librarians will want to consider how library policies might need adjustment to handle increased use of OER by teachers and students. Students, for example, could need access to the library after hours to use interactive OER that help them to

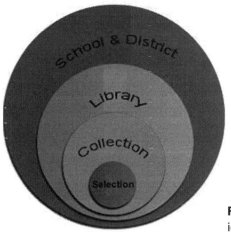

Figure 5.1. Layers of school librarians' policy considerations.

master science concepts. Library Internet connections could require re-evaluation to accommodate more simultaneous users. Teachers increasingly use projectors and interactive whiteboards to display OER, and students might use video or still cameras from the library's inventory to remix OER; library scheduling and access policies have to be adjusted to reflect such use.

The "Collection Development Policy" (CDP) is intended to be a living document that is frequently updated to reflect changing needs of the school as a community-based educational organization. This policy includes "a detailed description of a library's plans for developing and maintaining its collection of materials" (Pattee 2014, 22) that provides "a broad framework of how the library approaches its collection building and maintenance activities" (Evans and Zarnosky Saponaro 2012, 71).

Data Considerations

Many policy elements require ongoing data collection for implementation. Table 5.1 illustrates policy components; the items in bold are supported and informed by data.

As Table 5.1 shows, the policies share many comment data–informed elements. Regardless of which policy style is followed, when STEM OER are integrated into the collection, the librarian must ensure that STEM is a stated priority of the collection. Your STEM OER collection should be managed just like your print collection, such as by using the continuous review, evaluation, and weeding (CREW) approach (Bishop 2013).

In the case of a STEM collection that is being revitalized with STEM OER, be sure that the policy includes coverage, age, and size targets for the STEM collection as well as preferred formats. Selection procedures include the considerations covered in Table 4.1 and, as starting points, refer to trusted sources such as the National Science Digital Library (NSDL), OER Commons, and other sources mentioned in this book.

As with the print collection, procedures should be in place to weed the collection. The STEM OER weeding process follows the weeding principles of "MUSTIE."

- **M**isleading and/or factual inaccuracies
- **U**gly—Worn out beyond mending or rebinding
- **S**uperseded by a new edition or better source

Table 5.1. Components of School Library, Collection, and Selection Policies

Library (Bishop, 2013)	Collection (Evans & Saporanaro, 2013)	Collection (Pattee, 2014)	Selection (Bishop, 2013)
Community and school analyses	Link to library and school policies	Statement of purpose	Selection philosophy
Library philosophy and mission statement	Description of library service communities	Library mission, goals, and objectives	Selection objectives
School library goals and objectives	**Goals for collection**	Description of library service communities	Selection responsibility
Programs and service descriptions	**Subject areas or formats included in the library collection**	Description of budgeting or funding for collection	Selection criteria
Personnel job descriptions	Selection responsibility	Selection responsibility	Gifts
Selection policies and procedures	**Special criteria for selection**	**Subjects and formats included in the library collection**	Policies on controversial materials
Acquisition, processing, and cataloging procedures	Relationship to other public and school libraries in the area	**Selection and evaluation criteria**	Reconsideration policy
Gifts	**Evaluation and disposal procedures**	**Maintenance and weeding criteria and procedures**	**Selection procedures**
Maintaining materials and equipment	Gifts and donations	Gift policies	
Inventory of materials	Complaint procedures	Evaluation and inventory procedures	
Weeding materials		Intellectual freedom statements	
Circulation		Complaint procedures	
Library record confidentiality		Policy versioning procedures	
Collection evaluation			
Internet and technology policies			
Copyright and fair use compliance			
Intellectual freedom			

- **Trivial**—No discernible literary or scientific value
- **Irrelevant** to the needs and interests of your community
- **Elsewhere**—Easily obtained from another source

STEM materials are especially sensitive to criteria 1 and 3, because scientific concepts often can be misunderstood and scientific discoveries can update facts quickly. Materials in STEM areas tend to stay current for about five years (Bishop 2013). The STEM OER that are candidates for weeding based on age can be identified by using collection-analysis tools such as Follett's *TitleWise*—this is an additional advantage of including OER in a catalog.

Link checking also can be a source of weeding information. Clicking each link in a catalog, however, can be a laborious process. Tools such as *InfoWorks Link Checker 2.0*[1] can be used to detect and check the links in the catalog. The tool generates a report to use to reconcile the changed and dead links. Another method is to create a separate document listing the links used to create records and then link checking that document using free software such as *LinkChecker.*[2]

Promoting a STEM Collection

Formal and informal surveys of the school community also can provide essential sources of data that not only assess a collection, but also can help promote it. In recent years there has been a growing awareness that usage and implementation "paradata," such as ratings, annotations, and user reviews are needed to properly curate the content in repositories and determine resource suitability for teaching and learning tasks. As Griffin (Rosenbaum 2011) pointed out, "Subjective reviews submitted from highly qualified educators as well as independent reviewers are valuable elements that could be, and should be, included as unique data . . ." (para. 3). Features that capture other aspects of the user experience such as incidences as favoriting, sharing, viewing, and downloading also aid catalog assessment (Griffin 2013). Cataloging resources gives users the ability to comment on OER records, thus helping identify which resources users prefer and what they are using the resources for.

In addition to "crowdsourced" aspects of data that can be used for evaluation and promotion, learners, teachers, administrators, and parents each have special considerations for OER promotion. For each stakeholder, the following sections review some general considerations and one specific implementation scenario that links to an *Empowering Learners* role and one of AASL's *Standards for the 21st-Century Learner*.

Promoting to Students

A major concept of curation is participation. It's easy to see how students might recommend or rate resources. Building on the idea of having students leave resource reviews on catalog records in Destiny,[3] students can be encouraged to post their reactions to OER directly on their favorite social media outlets. By allowing students to post via social media channels directly from the library catalog, as Follett *Library Connections* blogger Ruth Aptaker (2013, para. 2) says,

> [W]e show them that we are current and up to speed with the times. The less our students think of libraries as going the way of the dinosaur, the better. They will be more apt to come to us with their information needs and trust us as viable resources. Plus your library gets the added bonus of free advertisement!

Having the school library catalog act as a repository for metadata about student-created work that reflects OER use and reuse also can send a powerful message to users that they are valuable participants in library collection practices. The more often that students use the collection, the more opportunities there are to find out the types of STEM OER they find useful, and the more opportunities there are to promote AASL's *Standards for the 21st-Century Learner*.

Box 5.1. Buckets of Fun with Argument-Driven Inquiry, AASL Standard 2, and the Teacher Role

Argument-Driven Inquiry (ADI) is a learning approach that supports the Next Generation Science Standards (http://www.nextgenscience.org/). Rooted in the findings of the National Research Council's (NRC) *Taking Science to School* (NRC 2007, 28) stance that "learning to think scientifically is a matter of acquiring problem-solving strategies for coordinating theory and evidence, mastering counterfactual reasoning, distinguishing patterns of evidence that do and do not support a definitive conclusion, and understanding the logic of experimental design." ADI can help students gain science literacy by using argument structure, applying scientific reasoning, and communicating in the language of science. To learn more about ADI, check out some of the resources discussed below.

The second standard of the *Standards for the 21st-Century Learner* (AASL 2009a) calls for students to gain experience in the library that will allow them to "draw conclusions, make informed decisions, apply knowledge to new

---

situations, and create new knowledge. They should be able to use the writing process, media and visual literacy, and technology skills to create products that express new understandings."

ADI is perfect for library-based learning, but it is not a single library-visit activity nor does it need to be a sophisticated debate. The goal of ADI is to help students integrate their observations and the things they read in reputable sources (which, in ADI, is called "evidence") into explanations (which, in ADI, are called "arguments"). Rather, teachers can work with their school librarians—over a few days or even a week—to integrate the evidence from science activities that the teachers lead and the information-gathering activities that school librarians lead into arguments that students consider, agree with, or possibly reject.

For elementary students, a great entry point into ADI is the use of "evidence buckets." An evidence bucket is a group-created illustration (similar to those provided below) that reflects all of the information collected about a particular topic. Teachers and librarians can use evidence buckets with students to learn about, for example, the potential effects of warming ocean water and rising ocean levels.

To begin, be sure to explore the idea of evidence with students. Even the youngest students are likely to have heard the word before on television or in books. Encourage them to describe what they think evidence is. They might be most familiar with evidence as something used in court or by police in criminal investigations. This starting point can help students see that police and lawyers use evidence to explain why something happens, and that the person with the most and the best evidence is the person whose explanation usually prevails.

With the ideas of evidence and explanation in mind, facilitate small experiments in which students can observe phenomena relating to changes in air and water temperature. Have multiple groups of children working at once, starting with OER lessons from sites such as the National Oceanographic and Atmospheric Administration's (NOAA) *Ocean Temps,*[4] the National Center for Atmospheric Research's (NCAR) *Changing Planet: Rising Ocean Temperatures—Rising Sea Levels,*[5] or the U.S. Department of Energy, Atmospheric Radiation Measurement Climate Research Facility's *When Floating Ice Melts in the Sea.*[6]

As the students are completing their experiments, have them present their experiments and observations to the class. Students then can record their observations in an illustration of a bucket on a large chart posted on the wall. This illustration is their first evidence bucket.

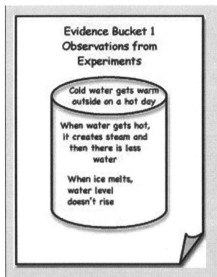

Figure 5.2. Sample observation evidence bucket poster.

Then, in the library, students can explore the complex interactions between the climate and oceans by viewing the National Aeronautics and Space Administration (NASA) video OER, *Oceans of Climate.*[7] Discuss the video with students in a large group or in small groups, and help the students gather and develop their observations about climate and oceans gleaned from the video. Students can add these ideas to a second evidence bucket.

On another day, teachers could choose to do another round of experiments and have students add to or remove things from their first evidence bucket. If possible, extend the time students have to gather information in the library about climate change. Direct kids to OERs from sites such as the University

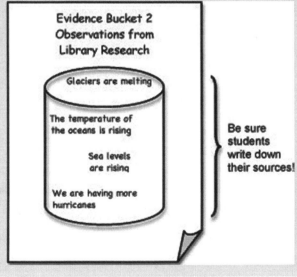

Figure 5.3. Sample library research evidence bucket poster.

Corporation for Atmospheric Research's (UCAR) *Water Water Everywhere*,[8] and the Environmental Protection Agency's (EPA) *Climate Change Kids*.[9] Be sure to have students include a reference to the information source when they add the information to the second bucket.

After everyone has contributed their experiment observations to the buckets, the teacher and librarian place the bucket illustrations side by side. Include a third piece of chart paper labeled "Explanations." Ask students to look at contents of both buckets and identify things that might be related, and to explain why they think they're related. As students interpret observations from each bucket and explain their reasoning, ask them to write their explanations to the third chart.

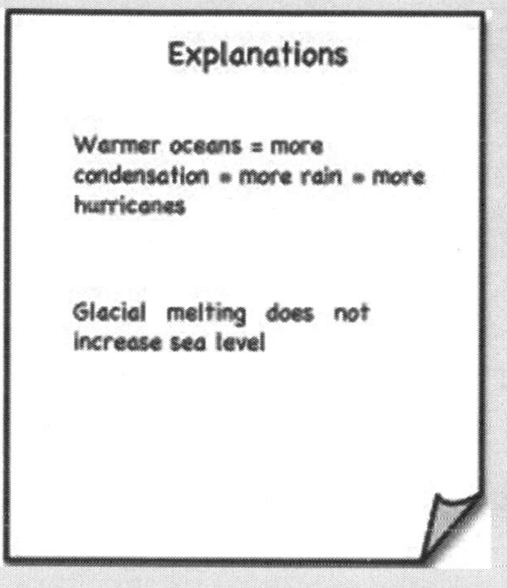

Explanations

Warmer oceans = more condensation = more rain = more hurricanes

Glacial melting does not increase sea level

Figure 5.4. Sample explanation evidence bucket poster.

Evidence buckets and argument presentations are powerful tools to help even the youngest students construct explanations related to scientific knowledge. They also are great tools to help students develop communication, information seeking, and synthesis skills. Later, teachers can build on this activity to help students use both direct and indirect evidence to make scientific arguments and to seek and synthesize a wider range of information sources. With OER, teachers and librarians have linked information literacy to science literacy!

Promoting to Teachers

Promoting STEM OER to teachers also can involve participation. Encouraging teachers to contribute plentiful, complete, and accurate reviews of resources, however, has proven to be difficult, despite the fact that many teachers report a favorable response to complete reviews left by other educators. Incentives rarely are effective because many teachers view feedback about their resource preferences as personal criticism. Teachers tend to be altruistically motivated and enthusiastic about sharing information about a resource when they feel the resource is valuable and would help other teachers (Griffin 2013; Khoo, Recker, and Marlino 2003).

The collection-evaluation process includes a number of ways that teachers can contribute to STEM OER curation. Dialogue with teachers about current resources that should be weeded and requests for replacement are obvious points of entry. Drawing links between STEM OER that support the AASL *Standards* and the *Next Generation Science Standards* also are ways to show teachers that instructional partnering events that use resources in the collection meet a range of learning needs.

Box 5.2. Taking Energy Inquiry Further with AASL Standard 1 and the Instructional Partner Role

For K–2 students, activities in the school library and with the school librarian should focus on helping students identify any questions they have about what they heard and saw. Often, these questions will be of a fact-finding nature, but some students might be ready to pose essential questions that, for example, use "how" or "why." As students seek information, work toward having them determine the point of view of authors and, if possible, compare the points of view to help students to understand differences. Finally, work with teachers to help students decide whether the information found is adequate to answer their questions. Enabling students to thoughtfully begin and conclude information tasks is fundamental to sound information-seeking skills.

In the library, for example, students could watch a short video clip about the sun from the television show *Nova*. This video can be viewed in the PBS LearningMedia[10] free educational multimedia database. At the conclusion of the video, ask students if—based on what they heard and saw in the video—they have any questions about the sun and its interaction with our climate. As students share their ideas, the school librarian can illustrate how the topics of student questions relate to the main idea of the sun using a concept mapping tool such as Kidspiration.[11] With guidance, students will see how their topics relate to the main idea, as well as how their ideas relate to one another in the concept map.

Work with individual students to find answers to their questions by referring to encyclopedias and other reference books as well as preselected age-appropriate Web resources. At the conclusion of the information-seeking

---

process, work with students to determine whether their questions have been answered and whether strategies for further information seeking are necessary. After the students have completed their information-seeking task, they can come back together as a group and report their responses. Referring back to the concept map created earlier, the school librarian can add the answers to the diagram of the questions while teachers help students to identify the relationship between the answers.

The basic activity for K–2 students outlined above also can be adapted for students in grades 3–5. The upper-elementary students can discern questions that require facts from essential questions that require deeper investigation through brainstorming to identify main parts of the topic and questions that cannot be answered easily. At this level, many students are able to independently determine whether their information represents divergent viewpoints and even might be able to intentionally seek information that represents multiple points of view. Students, with some guidance, also should be able to determine whether the information located is adequate for the question under investigation.

Promoting to Parents and the Community

Parents view using technology and digital resources as an essential element of college and career readiness (Project Tomorrow 2014) as well as a way in which they can engage with students' learning activities outside of the school building and beyond the school day (Project Tomorrow 2012a). Parents also view children's interest in STEM as a personal and national priority (Project Tomorrow and PASCO Scientific 2008).

When STEM learning occurs through multimedia rich imagery, students are more able to grasp and apply scientific concepts (Boster et al. 2007; Schwan and Riempp 2004; Yerrick, Ross, and Molebash, 2003–2004). Even still and printed images can have dramatic effects on student learning. An essential and often under-recognized aspect of digital learning is the offline creativity it can inspire. With all of the focus on student achievement, children often lack opportunities to express their knowledge of classroom content with drawing and creation—activities that predominantly take place at home. Librarians can engage parent volunteers, home-schooling parents, or even parents in their homes to help students engage with visual STEM OER and create artifacts of their understanding.

Box 5.3. (Lap)book 'Em! Getting Creative with Science Lapbooks, AASL Standard 4, and the Leader Role

Many teachers have embraced science notebooking as a way for students to record their learning experiences and observational data. Some students—such as the student who created the notebook shown below—use the opportunity to add their own illustrations to show their learning. Science notebooking is an incredibly rich activity that brings together reading, writing, reflection, and other modes of expression.

Using AASL's Standard 4, school librarians help students pursue personal and aesthetic growth in the school library by:

- Encouraging students to read widely and fluently to make connections with self, the world, and previous reading;

- Seeking information for personal learning in a variety of formats and genres;

- Connecting ideas to their own interests, previous knowledge, and experience;

- Demonstrating motivation by seeking information to answer personal questions and interests;

- Trying a variety of formats and genres;

- Displaying a willingness to go beyond academic requirements; and

- Interpreting new information based on cultural and social context.

Lapbooking applies the variety, interactivity, and personalization of scrapbooking to science notebooking. The *Lapbooking 101* blog[12] describes it as:

> [A]n inexpensive portfolio or collection of mini-books, flaps, and folded display material, that provides interactive space for drawings, stories, graphs, graphics, timelines, diagrams, and written work, from any topic, unit study, book you choose, gathered, glued, and creatively displayed in a colored standard sized cardboard folder, often folded in a "shutter-fold" that fits in your lap.

It's easy to get started with lapbooking. (The "Taking it Further" section of this chapter contains links to images of lapbooks.) File folders form the base. Construction paper can be used any number of ways. Students can create and attach pockets in which additional creations can be placed. They could use construction paper for flaps that can be flipped up or out to display additional information. Children also can attach illustrations that they create, combine, or cut from online image OER repositories, and include explanatory text for each of the items they include that give the lapbook reader an idea of sequence or coherence. Scissors, markers, crayons, removable glue, and removable tape also are must-have items for lapbooking!

After the supplies are gathered and ready to use, make sure that students are familiar with the idea of a lapbook. Perhaps show or have students look at an online collection of lapbooks[13] to see some of the many different ways that lapbooks can be constructed.

It might be helpful to have students plan the layout of their lapbooks using a "storyboard"-type structure. This roadmap helps to ensure that students think about the important concepts. Students can use a template for the lapbook layout but, if possible, let students use their own judgment and creativity to develop their own layouts. The folder can be "shutter" folded so that the cover opens on each side to reveal the contents, or created directly using the file folder to create a single-flap cover opening to one large area for contents. A student, for example, might draw storyboards for a lapbook about the water cycle that looks like Figure 5.5 on the outside, and looks like Figure 5.6 on the inside.

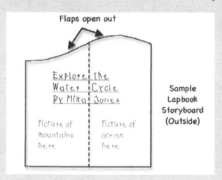

Figure 5.5. Sample lapbook storyboard outside view.

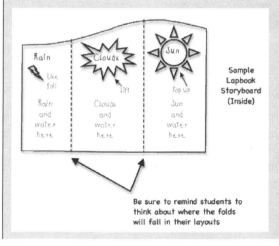

Figure 5.6. Sample lapbook storyboard inside view.

Although lapbooking can be used at the end of a unit for students to demonstrate what they learned, it can also be using during a unit for students to record learning "as it happens," much like they would do in science notebooking. This application doesn't require a storyboard, but teachers likely will need to encourage students to be creative in how they add or rearrange items (hence using removable tape or glue) to their lapbooks if they begin to run out of room.

Lapbooking activities in the school library also provide an important opportunity to connect time in the dynamic online image databases. When lapbooking is also used with school library activities—such as learning to use reference books or online encyclopedias—it can be a powerful way to nurture student creativity and promote aesthetic appreciation for artistic expression. Students can use pictures from free databases such as the Metropolitan Museum of Art's freely downloadable OER collection[14] as inspirations for their illustrations, cut articles and photos out of newspapers and magazines, and print photos from approved online sources to enhance their creations.

The school library's space also lends itself to a number of activities that enhance the use of lapbooks. The school library probably also has many tables and has room to spread out—ideal for active lapbookers! Because the bases for lapbooks are file folders, they are easy to organize, collect, and exchange. A hanging file folder box is a great portable tool for keeping lapbooks at hand.

By definition, lapbooks are personally designed and created, so they are great tools for differentiation. When used with science notebooking, learners having a range of reading, writing, and drawing skills can combine text, pictures, illustrations, and other personal additions to show what they know. When teachers lapbook with school librarians, it provides the camaraderie, space, and time to take the activity in a number of enriching directions. Lapbooking is very versatile and creative—the only limits are the students' imaginations!

Promoting to Administrators

The STEM OER appeal to administrators for many reasons. Open educational resources help to control instructional materials costs; justify technology and bandwidth expenditures; demonstrate learning innovation to parents and community members; and engage students more deeply (Hewlett Foundation 2013). By personalizing their learning experiences with OER, students can better communicate their understandings verbally and demonstrate their knowledge through a variety of media (Office of Educational Technology 2013). Showcases of student mastery in the library can engage administrators in the "return on investment" that STEM OER can bring to the school community.

A study sponsored by the Hewlett Foundation (Boston Consulting Group 2013), however, suggested that far fewer school administrators than teachers and students are aware of the benefits of OER for learning. Yet school administrators set policy and standards that enable effective OER implementation, and have responsibility to document learning outcomes within the school environment (Boston Consulting Group 2013); school administrator awareness and support for OER is absolutely essential for a data-driven personalized learning environment (Manderson 2012).

Box 5.4. A Science Fair Makeover in the School Library with AASL Standard 3 and the Information Specialist Role

The National Science Teachers' Association (NSTA) reported that 75% of its surveyed members reported hosting a science fair each school year (NSTA 2011). Although many educators value science fairs as opportunities for students to explore new ideas, apply and develop new skills, and demonstrate their learning, an effective and interesting science fair can be challenging to pull off! With the help of OER and the AASL Standards, however, school librarians in their role as information specialist can help students "share knowledge and participate ethically and productively as members of our democratic society." Science fairs can be events that engage the entire school and showcase the positive outcomes of inquiry-based learning in the context of state and local standards. In the case of a science fair, AASL Standard 3 to "Inquire, think critically, and gain knowledge" can be supported by the use and creation of OER.

School librarians have long histories with science fairs. Many school librarians report that science fair project idea materials are key components of their science collections (Mardis and Hoffman 2007b) and that the science fair is a great opportunity for connecting with science teachers (Mardis 2007). School librarians have much to offer a science fair. A study of children's questions to the Internet Public Library (IPL)[15] (http://ipl.org) virtual reference service showed that students in third to eighth grade primarily ask science homework questions about science fairs. Their questions are not just about science fair topics; students want to know how to conduct science experiments and how to display results (Mardis 2008). Another study showed that when children do not understand how to conduct their science fair experiments, their parents take over (Watson 2003).

Students and teachers have found science fair participation particularly frustrating because the topics range widely and it's difficult to organize projects on so many different topics. Using the NGSS Disciplinary Core Ideas as a guide, librarians can develop a theme for the science fair and work closely with science teachers to ensure that this focus is reflected in the students' topics and in the library collection.

Step 1. Use OER to help children to understand why the science fair is important.

Although this step seems obvious, many science teachers do not spend adequate time helping their students understand why the science fair is an important part of their learning.

Although videos such as "Treeline Elementary's Fourth Grade Science Fair,"[16] the clever Mrs. Hunt's "Science Fair Hints"[17] from New Zealand, or Christine Little's "Why Participate in a Science Fair?"[18] presentation can help students envision the outcome of their projects, it's always helpful to help the entire school community understand what a tremendous opportunity the science fair can be to make friends and learn about future careers.

The *Science News for Kids* article, "The Science Fair Circuit,"[19] shows students how the science fair can become an activity that they can enjoy throughout their school years, and even can use as a way to get to know people across the country and to secure valuable college scholarships. Sources such as the IPL's "Why Should I Do a Science Fair Project?"[20] can help set expectations and build excitement.

Step 2. Identify an appropriate topic and a testable question for the science fair project.

As most science teachers know, the Internet teems with sites that list many project ideas for science fairs. Be sure to check the great directory of science fair idea sites at the IPL.[21]

Helping children choose their questions for science fair projects is an area where the library's collection can shine! The AASL standards emphasize that the ability to phrase compelling questions is a key part of learning in the library. The answers generated by productive questions are derived from first-hand experiences and raise children's awareness that there can be more than one correct answer to a question. Productive questions cannot be answered with a simple "yes" or "no" because they require children to test theories through attention, focus, measuring or counting, comparison, action, problem solving, or reasoning before responding—features of a great science fair project. A good question focuses work on the rest of the science fair project; background research is easier to conduct, results are easier to analyze, and conclusions come more naturally.

Testable questions include the following.[22]

- **Measuring and Counting Questions.** Quantitative questions encourage sharp observations and communication. Carefully phrased measuring and counting questions help students organize their thinking and unify similar concepts or ideas through the use of grouping or sets. Students use the science process skills of measuring and classifying as they check accuracy and use new instruments. Examples of measuring and counting questions include: "How many. . . ?", "How often. . . ?", "How long. . . ?", and "How much. . . . ?"

- **Comparison Questions.** Comparison questions ask students to identify number relationships, develop concepts of alike and different, quantify the number of ways things are alike or different, and describe how things fit together. The science processes of observing, measuring, classifying, and communicating are used by students as they answer comparison questions. Comparison question starters include: "How do . . . fit together?"; "How are . . . different?"; "In how many ways are . . . alike?"; and "In how many ways do . . . differ?"

- **Action Questions.** Action questions involve students in the science process skills of predicting, investigating, and experimenting. Finding the answers to "What happens if . . . ?" and "What would happen if you . . . ?" engages students in the process of inquiry to discover an answer through investigation and experimentation. Asking students to make predictions about the outcomes of investigations or experiments stimulates thinking about variables, hypotheses, and conclusions that affect the investigation before it begins.

Often, choosing the right question is a matter of rephrasing a weak question. The Discovery Channel's Science Fair Central website[23] provides great examples of questions that are rephrased from unproductive to testable productive questions.

Step 3. Review the scientific method and processes for conducting science experiments.

A good science fair project, however, involves much more than a topic. Grasp of the process is important for making the science fair an experience that translates to other learning activities. A question that can be investigated through a clearly defined process designed to result in logical conclusions is essential.

Step 4. Ground the topic in appropriate research and references.

This step often is overlooked in many science fair experiments, but grounding the questions driving the science experiment in known research is an essential part of drawing conclusions from collected data. For a science fair, librarians might want to focus on the location of information within preselected books and websites and allow students to focus on analysis and synthesis of information. Note that each of these sources includes both text and pictures, and most are of an appropriate independent reading level.

With help from the teachers, school librarian, or parents, students can locate OERs such as "Talking Trees: A Living Diary of Climate"[24] from the National Science Foundation's *Why Files.* Imagine how long it would take to help students find appropriate resources like these for each of their projects using a Web search engine!

Give students independent time to review their resources and write down one or two main ideas from each source. Schedule one-on-one meetings during library time for teachers and school librarians to meet with students to review notes on sources and make sure that each student has a clearly defined question and good background sources. Be sure that students record their sources in a bibliography in formats such as those presented on the *Science Buddies* website[25] or with Web-based formatting tools such as the free and easy-to-use *NoodleBib Express.*[26]

Step 5. Conduct the experiment and gather data.

Spreadsheets and photos can be great ways to record data, but OER such as the interactives in the Vermillion Parish (Louisiana) Schools are great for numerical data recording and analysis.[27]

Step 6. Analyze data and draw conclusions.

Of course, data analysis depends on the project. For this phase, teachers and school librarians could check in with students as they collect and analyze their data, providing what library guru Joan Frye Williams calls "bookend service" (Mardis 2011). That is, check in with the students as they get started, then occasionally as they work, and again at the end of their activity to ensure that they are comfortable with the process.

Although different research processes word them in different ways, drawing conclusions for a research question really is the result of the simple formula shown below.

A *(findings of prior research; known facts)* + **B** *(finding from experiment)* = **C** *(conclusion)*

Be sure students emphasize that conclusions can affirm prior research, refute prior research, or present unexpected conclusions. Not all experiments result in "yes" or "no" answers.

Step 7. Display and communicate research findings in a clear format.

The school librarian can be a valuable partner here regardless of whether students are to present their work on a traditional tabletop triptych or use a multimedia method such as Glogster[28] for multimedia posters or Prezi[29] for presentations. Digital formats provide artifacts to catalog and share with administrators, parents, and other students.

The school librarian is an important contributor to the value of a science fair. As information specialists working toward AASL Standard 3 with OER, the science fair can be—as one Prezi creator noted—"Not Your Mother's Science Fair."[30]

Notes

1. *InfoWorks Link Checker 2.0.* http://www.itcompany.com/linkcheck.html.

2. *Link Checker.* http://wummel.github.io/linkchecker/.

3. *Destiny.* http://legacyhelp.fsc.follett.com/Content/patrons/patron_tools/ addreviewform_overview.htm.

4. National Oceanographic and Atmospheric Administration's (NOAA). *Ocean Temps.* http://www.oar.noaa.gov/k12/html/oceantemps2.html.

5. National Center for Atmospheric Research (NCAR). "Changing Planet: Rising Ocean Temperatures—Rising Sea Levels." http://www.windows2universe.org/ teacher_resources/ocean_tempera tures.html.

6. Atmospheric Radiation Measurement Climate Research Facility. "When Floating Ice Melts in the Sea." http://education.arm.gov/teacherslounge/lessons/When-Floating-Ice-Melts-in-the-Sea-Gr-K-2.pdf?id=20.

7. NASA. "Oceans of Climate." http://www.nasa.gov/mp4/332473main_earth-20090421-320.mp4.

8. University Corporation for Atmospheric Research (UCAR). "Water Water Everywhere." http://www.eo.ucar.edu/kids/wwe/index.htm.

9. Environmental Protection Agency (EPA). *Climate Change Kids.* http://www.epa.gov/climatechange/kids/.

10. PBS LearningMedia. http://pbslearningmedia.org.

11. "Kidspiration." http://www.inspiration.com/Kidspiration.

12. "Lapbooking 101." http://lapbooking.wordpress.com/.

13. http://tinyurl.com/43de5n8.

14. Metropolitan Museum of Arts. Downloadable OER Collection. http://www.metmuseum.org/ collection/the-collection-online.

15. Internet Public Library (IPL). http://ipl.org.

16. "Treeline Elementary's Fourth Grade Science Fair," http://www1 .teachertube.com/ viewVideo.php?video_id=107527&title =Treeline_Elementary_Fourth_Grade_Science_Fair.

17. "Science Fair Hints." http://mrshunt.glogster.com/.

18. "Why Participate in a Science Fair?" http://prezi.com/ a8-zygjnbgw9/why-participate-in-a-science-fair/.

19. *Science News for Kids* article, "The Science Fair Circuit." http:// www.sciencenewsforkids.org/2006/10/the-science-fair-circuit-3/.

20. Internet Public Library. "Why Should I Do a Science Fair Project?" http://www.ipl.org/div/ projectguide/gettingstarted.html#whyscifair.

21. Internet Public Library. http://www.ipl.org/div/projectguide/ choosingatopic.html.

22. http://www.maisk-6scienceinquiry.org/questions.htm.

23. Discovery Channel. "Science Fair Central." http://school.discovery education.com/ sciencefaircentral/Getting-Started/Investigation.html.

24. "Talking Trees: A Living Diary of Climate." http://whyfiles.org/ 021climate/ringers.html.

25. "Science Buddies." http://www.sciencebuddies.org/mentoring/ project_bibliography.shtml.

26. "NoodleBib Express." http://noodletools.com/login.php.

27. http://www.vrml.k12.la.us/cc/tools/tools.htm.

28. Glogster. http://glogster.com

29. Prezi. http://prezi.com.

30. "Not Your Mother's Science Fair." http://prezi.com/yzl7ich1dqtj/ not-your-mothers-science-fair/.

Taking it Further

More about Argument-Driven Inquiry

Berland, L. K. and B. J. Reiser. 2011. "Classroom Communities' Adaptations of the Practice of Scientific Argumentation." *Science Education* 95: 191–216. doi: 10.1002/sce.20420.

Kulthau, C.C. 2010. "Guided Inquiry: School Libraries and the 21st Century." *School Libraries Worldwide* 16 (1): 17–28.

Sampson, V., J. Grooms, and J. Walker. 2009. "Argument-Driven Inquiry: A Way to Promote Learning During Laboratory Activities." *The Science Teacher* 76 (7): 42–47.

Zembal-Saul, C. 2009. "Learning to Teach Elementary School Science as Argument." *Science Education* 93: 687–719. doi: 10.1002/sce.20325.

More about Lapbooking

All About HS Curriculum. "Lapbooking and Notebooking." Accessed September 8, 2014. http://www.pinterest.com/hscurriculum/lapbooking-notebooking/.

Hazard, Theresa. *Lap Books.* Accessed September 8, 2014. http://www.pinterest.com /hscurriculum/lapbooking-notebooking/.

Jazzy. *Lapbooks.* Accessed September 8, 2014. http://www.pinterest.com/jazzy_027/lapbooks/.

Jimmiehomeschoolmom. Lapbook image set 1. Accessed August 7, 2014. http://tinyurl.com /3kpet74.

Jimmiehomeschoolmom. Lapbook image set 2. Accessed August 7, 2014. http://tinyurl.com /3hl7bxb.

Lapbooking 101. "What is Lapbooking?" 2008. Accessed August 7, 2014. http://lapbooking.wordpress.com/lapbook/.

Master Lap Book List. Access September 8, 2014. http://www.home schoolshare.com /index_lapbooks_list.php.

More about Student Involvement in Collection Development

Georgia superstar school librarian, Buffy Hamilton, has created a very complete presentation: "Inviting Student Participation in Your School Library Media Program." Accessed August 7, 2014. http://theunquietlibrarian.wikispaces.com/student-participation.

More about Implementing Open Educational Resources

OER 101. A series of iTunesU video, audio, and text course modules about finding and using OER. Co-created by Illinois school librarian, Josh Mika, a 2011 Apple Distinguished Educator. Modules include the following.

- A Guide to Digital Research (ePub text)
- A Guide to Digital Research (PDF text)

- Designing Creative Research Projects (text)
- Diigo (Video)
- EasyBib (Video)
- Formulating a Thesis Statement (text)
- Google Scholar (text)
- Introduction to Digital Research (Video)
- Website Evaluation (text)
- Website Evaluation Checklist (text)
- Wikipedia—The Research Launching Pad (text)

CHAPTER 6

Summary and Conclusion

An Open Letter to School Librarians and Science Educators

Introduction

This book examines the exciting opportunities that science, technology, engineering, and mathematics (STEM) open educational resources (OER) present for school librarians. It also discusses how school librarians' expertise in selecting, describing, promoting, and managing (i.e., curating) physical *and* digital collections can propel learning communities to meet the demands of common standards through cutting-edge, equal access, dynamic, and high-quality digital learning.

Benefits of Open Educational Resources

Open education resources are learning materials in the public domain that educators and students are permitted to access, share, and modify to customize and personalize learning and teaching. The knowledge-sharing enabled by OER consumption and creation, and improved access to a wide range of multimedia resources can foster college and career readiness through better education. Creating, sharing, and reusing OER decreases the costs of instructional and learning materials. These savings are particularly important given the limited budgets of states, districts, and schools. Importantly, OER maximize and best leverage the important work of publicly funded STEM research and education organizations such as the National Aeronautics and Space Administration, the National Science Foundation, and the National Oceanographic and Atmospheric Administration. Open educational resources also eliminate the delays associated with securing permission to use existing digital materials by allowing educators to freely use open materials without having to secure copyright clearance. School administrators then are able to shift resources into onsite expertise to build and maintain OER collections, and into time and resources for professional development in technology and STEM content development.

Open educational resources give students access to supplemental learning resources that enhance their ability to engage in independent learning and to pursue learning aligned with personal interests. These educational resources provide a pathway toward ensuring that every student has access to high-quality, engaging, personalized, and up-to-date content at school and at home. When students engage deeply with OER to demonstrate their learning, these efforts can showcase district, school, and teacher leadership in content creation and customization. OER can serve as a tool for engaging students, parents, and communities and highlighting the opportunities available to students who learn through open content.

Challenges for Open Educational Resources

There are at least two main barriers to OER policy implementation: lack of funding to support OER development and oversight, and lack of funding for marketing and promotion of OER. Policymakers have pointed to a lack of teacher experience, curation staff, and the support necessary to enable schools to take full advantage of the learning transformation OER offer.

The second barrier to OER policy implementation relates to the differences between how OER developers promote their content as compared to how traditional publishers market their materials. In general, funding for OER is dedicated to content development with little remaining for marketing and outreach. Because teachers struggle to find OER on the Web or even to find time to sort through vast collections such as those listed in this book's appendixes, having an expert curator who can assess the community's readiness to engage with OER in the school is essential. Figure 6.1 illustrates three possible scenarios for OET implementation proposed to the Hewlett Foundation (Boston Consulting Group 2013).

	OER enriches existing resources	OER used as primary material	OER helps "flip" classroom
Role of OER	OER reinforces existing content, but remains supplementary • E.g., teachers use standard textbook but assign Khan videos as homework	OER primary instructional material in the classroom • Teachers start by using off-the-shelf OER products, then remix and share their own content	OER allows for individualized in-classroom learning • Personalized content delivered via learning platforms • OER significant portion of overall content
Role of teacher	Teacher engages in some remixing and sharing of content Teaching methods remain largely the same	Teacher remixes and shares content Teaching methods remain largely the same	Teacher remixes and shares content Teacher serves as coach rather than lecturer
Level of disruption	Low	Medium	High

Figure 6.1. Open educational resources implementation levels.

As Figure 6.1 shows, school communities can have low, medium, or high levels of readiness for OER. Open educational resources collection marketing, implementation guidance, and ongoing curation support can lead the school community to deeper levels of integration.

Science, Technology, Engineering, Mathematics, and Standards

Although barriers certainly exist, there also are many opportunities for OER policy creation and implementation to provide more efficient and effective school and library practices. In particular, the adoption of the Common Core State Standards (CCSS) and Next Generation Science Standards by more than half of U.S. states provides STEM educators a chance to reconsider their sources and strategies around instructional materials. There currently is a great need for CCSS-aligned content, and the OER community has begun to retool existing content and produce new materials. School administrators should consider building and library policies that make it easy for their teachers and librarians to vet and adopt such content. Additionally, national efforts are underway to organize a consortium of states to participate in a collaborative effort to develop even more CCSS- and NGSS-aligned STEM OER; however, STEM teachers still require implementation support.

If "scientifically based research" and "adequate yearly progress" were the rallying cries for education policy over the past eight years, then the new calls of the Obama era are for "connection," "motivation," and "innovation." As new policies are unveiled, it is clear that they represent a break from a single-minded focus on decisions based on student achievement data–derived studies in which students are randomly assigned to either control or experimental groups. The new national focus on educational innovation means marrying practical knowledge and lifelong relevance with observable gains in student learning. Although policies favorable toward OER development and adoption have the potential to save schools a great deal of money, a revolution in the learning environment is crucial for delivering personalized learning experiences for engaging students, and to potentially impact student outcomes when OER that is aligned with the CCSS and NGSS are used.

In this time of change in our society, children's needs, preferences, and interactions with the world are changing. These changes have sent education policymakers scrambling toward two extremes. The first extreme—a focus on testing and basic skills—seeks to ensure that all students leave school with equal knowledge and preparation for the workplace. The other extreme focuses on affective goals of helping children become good stewards of the environment, conscious participants in a democratic society, and technology-enabled individuals with dispositions that allow them to weather personal, economic, and cultural challenges. Nowhere else in schools is the tension between these two approaches to education seen more starkly than in science education, and no other context is more underappreciated as a revolutionizing force in science learning than school libraries.

Open Educational Resources, STEM, and the School Library Collection

Building science collections has proven particularly challenging for many school librarians who struggle with collection development in science because they lack formal education in that discipline. Scientific information changes very quickly and the content in published books often is outdated before the books can be placed on library shelves. As a result, staying abreast of developments in science to maintain a current collection probably is the most daunting task a media specialist faces.

Science books as old as 40 years have been found on many school library shelves (Mardis and Hoffman 2007a). Many school librarians do not feel confident about selecting science materials and, due to lack of both expertise and funds, often are left to tolerate old and inherited science collections to an extent that affects many school librarians' willingness and abilities to forge relationships with science teachers (Mardis 2007). Despite this difficult situation school librarians recognize the need to infuse their collections with more digital resources and, lacking funds to add more up-to-date periodicals, reference materials, databases, and video resources (Everhart, Mardis, and Johnston 2011), are open to OER. Librarians have cautioned that although non-book media such as streaming video have the potential to address deficiencies in science book collections with current, dynamic, and affordable open content materials, the school must have adequate bandwidth and equipment (Mardis 2009).

Although collection development in science can be challenging, collaboration between science teachers and school librarians can be even more so. Even though many science teachers struggle to find high-quality science resources, they are not always aware that school librarians can help them locate digital as well as print science resources (Mardis 2004). Additionally, science teachers do not perceive the school librarian as someone who could help them engage their computer-savvy students with interactive, visual, and up-to-date science resources (Schultz-Jones and Ledbetter 2009).

At a time when our nation does not have enough scientists to meet national needs, our children presently are not inspired to learn about science. Collections and collaborations to motivate more and better science learning are needed, and we must look ahead in this vital area to see what the future can offer as solutions to these problems.

What's Ahead with OER and STEM for School Librarians?

Our technology-rich and interest-poor children must be connected to new ways to become excited about science. The stakes for engaging students with STEM OER collections are high because a number of key learning trends rely on students' information and STEM fluencies.

These trends are united by their reliance on cyberinfrastruture. "Cyber-infrastructure" is a term first used by the National Science Foundation (NSF 2007) and typically is used to refer to information technology systems that provide particularly powerful and advanced capabilities. The word "cyberinfrastructure" intentionally is based on the word "infra-structure." This is because it provides a framework and a network to support twenty-first century learning by connecting existing and developing new Internet and data resources to extend the impact of scientific inquiry and outcomes to researchers, educators, and learners.

Cyberinfrastructure links computing systems, data, information resources, high-speed broadband networking, digitally enabled sensors, instruments, virtual organizations, and observatories with software services and tools to move thinking outside of the traditional learning model of teachers instructing students in classrooms or labs. Cyberinfrastructure learning environments encompass classrooms, laboratories, libraries, galleries, museums, zoos, workplaces, and many other locations. When cyberinfrastructure is implemented widely in education, preschool, K–12, and college will be interconnected in an open learning world in which learning is a routine part of life, and people learn throughout their lives. Cyber-enabled STEM learning trends that involve OER and are of particular interest to school librarians include the following.

Informal Learning

Informal learning is a burgeoning field that operates across a broad range of venues including museums, state parks, and after-school programs. Although informal learning can be organized around a number of topics such as fine arts, community building, and sports, informal science education presently is a very active area, especially as it can be used to increase students' interest in scientific phenomena, science careers, and ecological awareness. In a future linked through cyberinfrastructure, formal and informal learning environments will be connected, eliminating the disconnected feel of physically removed field trips. The Exploratorium in San Francisco's Center for Informal Learning and Schools has a great website about informal science education (http:// cils.exploratorium.edu/cils/).

Massive Open Online Courses

Massive open online courses (MOOC) and widespread online learning are trends that are picking up momentum in K–12 education. Many states and countries have passed mandatory online learning requirements (Barbour et al. 2011) and school librarians long have supported these learners in fully online and hybrid environments (Lamb and Callison 2005). Now, MOOCs are offering free learning opportunities to enormous numbers of simultaneous learners, and K–12 educators are looking to the combination of open content, learning analytics, standards-based curriculum, and personalized instruction as a way to supplement and enhance their current curriculum with courses that typically would not be available (Jackson 2013). School librarians can work with teachers to use a MOOC as a mini-unit in their classes, or as an after-school project. Every time a teacher has students engage in open content mini-courses, such as using lectures or content from YouTube or TED talks, in effect they are participating in a customized MOOC. Librarians also can facilitate teacher MOOC use for professional development. Leading MOOC provider, Coursera (https://www.coursera.org/courses?cats=teacherpd), for example, offers free professional development courses for K–12 teachers on topics such as evolution, ecology, and assessing twenty-first-century skills.

Crowdsourcing and Citizen Science

Crowdsourcing and citizen science engages volunteers in the collection of data, such as ecological information. In citizen science projects students not only do the "grunt work" of collecting data that scientists can analyze to chart ecological trends, they also participate in the inquiry process by connecting phenomena to data and to changes in the environment. Citizen science enables students to connect their desire to be environmentally aware and tech savvy, and helps to find ways to connect in-school and out-of-school activities to important global issues.

Citizen science projects use the Internet, texting, smartphones, tablets, and other Web 2.0 technologies to gather information about the environment. These technologies enable data collection for agencies and organizations dedicated to the protection and study of the environment and promote the use of kid-native, often unused-in-school technologies in fun, relevant, and service-oriented lessons involving science, math, and other curriculum areas. In the Neighborhood Nestwatch program (http://nationalzoo.si.edu /ConservationAndScience/MigratoryBirds/Research/Neighborhood_Nestwatch/), for example, volunteers work with scientists to find, observe, and compare bird nests in urban, suburban, and rural backyards. The results of participant observations already have yielded valuable information about the West Nile virus, lead contamination, songbird tracking, house wren behavior, and nest predation. Undoubtedly, the program also has inspired many of its student volunteers to become birdwatchers, ornithologists, or scientists in other fields.

Begin Where You Are

The AASL *Standards for the 21st-Century Learner* and *Empowering Learners: Guidelines for School Library Media Programs* are based on the principles that school libraries are more relevant than ever before, and are the ideal context for students to explore their own interests and connect their school life with the outside world. In this vein, science-learning trends provide a wealth of avenues for school libraries and librarians. Librarians now have the opportunity to bring forward skills that have been underemphasized, and can use aspects of their expertise to support innovative learning. The following sections provide some ways to take advantage of STEM OER in a school library.

Be a Broadband Specialist

The philosophy of cyberinfrastructure has much in common with the new AASL standards and guidelines. Teachers and administrators are cautious about using new resources because they fear that the network capacity will be outstripped. In many schools, this disconnect between perceived network capacity and actual network capacity became the responsibility of the school librarian to understand. It's in a librarian's best interest to alert science teachers of the cyberinfrastructure movement and the potential that robust broadband affords for creating an optimal learning environment. To make administrators and teachers aware of network capacity and future needs, start by checking network speed by using a tool such as CNET's Bandwidth Meter Online Speed Test (http://reviews.cnet.com/internet-speed-test/).

Clean Up the Print Science Collection and Diversify the Library's Catalog

The library's science collection probably has some "golden oldies" in the 000s, 500s, and 600s—get rid of them! Keeping them because the library can't afford to buy new books? Remember that STEM information older than seven years runs a very high risk of being inaccurate, so there's no reason to keep misinformation in the collection. Open educational resources are a great—usually free—way to freshen the science collection with resources that teachers probably don't know about and that students will enjoy. But finding OER is just a start. The resources must be findable to everyone else. Instead of maintaining a "link farm" on the school library website or compiling handouts that are instantly out of date, catalog the individual learning objects into the library catalog, the same way as a book or DVD. The metadata that comes with the learning objects provides most of the catalog record information and most learning objects have individual links, so users can access them directly through the OPAC. By cataloging them, the users can find the learning objects along with the books and videos in the collection.

Be a Policy Leader

Another aspect of cyberinfrastructure and use of OER is policy—school, library, collection, and selection. Ensure that the school library is wireless enabled, students and teachers can have more access to computer functions, and potentially bandwidth-intensive applications such as video can be used. To be part of the future of education—the future that is starting with STEM education—school librarians must be proactive in the policy-setting process. Be a fearless advocate of technologies you haven't mastered and be willing to understand that experimentation is part of the social learning process. If the librarian is willing to work with students to transmit data they collect over the Internet, use Web 2.0 applications to connect with the outside world, and create artifacts to demonstrate their knowledge, then the enthusiasm and energy created will help the more-timid teachers to understand the importance of technology leadership.

Participate and Create

If the school hasn't participated in a citizen science project such as the butterfly tracking Journey North project (http://www.learner.org/jnorth/) or Neighborhood Nestwatch (http://nationalzoo.si.edu/scbi/migratory-birds/research/neighborhood_nestwatch/), then start a citizen science project in your library and the libraries of nearby schools. Ask students to track birds or animals outside the library windows across seasons and exchange the information with other schools. The project can even be something as simple as having students research the houseplants or aquariums that many school librarians keep in their libraries, why people keep houseplants, and the plants' benefit to the environment. The project can include an exchange of information among schools within and beyond the district. Philodendrons and fish can be fascinating!

Appendix A
Starting Points for Locating Vetted K–12 STEM OER

Repository	URL
AAAS ScienceNetLinks	http://sciencenetlinks.com/
ActionBioscience.Org	http://www.actionbioscience.org/
Carnegie Mellon University	http://www.cmu.edu/oli/
CC Consortium for OER	http://oerconsortium.org/
CK-12 Foundation	http://www.ck12.org/flexr/
CodeAcademy	http://www.codecademy.com/
Creative Commons	http://creativecommons.org
Curriki	http://www.curriki.org/
Digital Learning Commons	http://www.learningcommons.org/
Digital Public Library of America (DPLA)	http://dp.la
Flatworld Knowledge	http://www.flatworldknowledge.com/
Getty Images	http://www.gettyimages.com/
HippoCampus	http://new.HippoCampus.org
ide@s	http://www.ideas.wisconsin.edu
Interactive Plasma Physics Education Experience (IPPEX)	http://ippex.pppl.gov
Internet Public Library (IPL)	http://ipl.org
Khan Academy	http://www.khanacademy.org/
Math Archives	http://archives.math.utk.edu/tutorials.html
MERLOT	http://www.merlot.org
Metropolitan Museum of Art	http://www.metmuseum.org/collection/the-collection-online
Michigan Online Resources for Educators (MORE)	http://more.mel.org
MIT Blossoms	http://blossoms.mit.edu

Mountain Heights Academy	http://www.mountainheightsacademy.org/
National Library of Virtual Manipulatives	http://nlvm.usu.edu/
National Science Digital Library	http://nsdl.org/
National Oceanographic and Atmospheric Administration (NOAA)	http://www.education.noaa.gov/
OER Commons	http://www.oercommons.org/
OER Policy Registry	http://wiki.creativecommons.org/OER_Policy_Registry
Open Courseware for High School	http://ocw.mit.edu/high-school/
Open Education Group	http://openedgroup.org
PhET	http://phet.colorado.edu/en/simulations/category/new
PBS LearningMedia	http://pbslearningmedia.org
Public Library of Science (PLoS)	http://www.plos.org
Rice Connexions	http://www.cnx.rice.edu
SAS® Curriculum Pathways®	http://www.sascurriculumpathways.com
Saylor Foundation	http://saylor.org
Smithsonian Seriously Amazing	http://seriouslyamazing.si.edu/
Teacher Tube	http://www.teachertube.com/
TEDEd	http://ed.ted.com/
Utah Education Network—Science	http://www.uen.org/k12educator/uenresources.php?cat=Science
WarneScience Science Café	http://www.sciencecafe.org.za/home
WatchKnowLearn	http://watchknowlearn.org
Wisc-Online	http://www.wisc-online.com/

Appendix B

K–12 STEM OER Collections with Downloadable Records Available Through the NSDL

Number of Records	Title	Description
38	A Mathematical Way to Think About Biology	This video collection is designed to help interdisciplinary scientists better understand biological systems using quantitative reasoning. In addition to a brief review of algebra and calculus, the collection includes basic introductions to modeling the dynamics of protein levels, population dynamics with cell-cell interactions, population dynamics with mutation, uncertainty analysis, stochastic dynamics, linear algebra, differential equations, and oscillations.
517	AMSER LAR Collection	AMSER LAR collection is composed of resources described for Learning Application Readiness (LAR).
13,806	AMSER: General Collection	AMSER is a portal of educational resources and services built specifically for those in community and technical colleges, but it is free for anyone to use.
206	Access Excellence @ The National Health Museum	This site contains bioscience classroom activities; teaching and learning strategies; health and bioscience news; a biotech section; a student resource section with science and math links; a visual library with graphics of life processes; the e-journal *Biology Education Online*; discussion boards; and health news, resources, and activities.
37	AlgoViz.org: The Algorithm Visualization Portal	AlgoViz.org is a gathering place and code repository for users and developers of algorithm visualizations (AVs), and is a gateway to AV-related services, collections, and resources. Visualizations are grouped by topic, and subjective evaluation data on the visualizations from a pedagogic perspective often is included. The site also provides links to research literature and allows users to share their visualizations.
650	American Museum of Natural History	The American Museum of Natural History in New York City is one of the world's preeminent scientific, educational, and cultural institutions. Its collections of online resources extend this reach by offering authoritative science content to educators and learners of all ages.

2660	Animal Diversity Web	Animal Diversity Web (ADW) is an online database of animal natural history, distribution, classification, and conservation biology hosted by the University of Michigan Museum of Zoology. Hundreds of hyperlinked pages and images illustrate the traits and general biology of these groups. It also offers thousands of species accounts that can include text, pictures, photographs, and movies of specimens and includes sound recordings.
20	Ask a Biologist	Explore the world of biology and meet biologists. This site helps pre-K through Grade 12 students, instructors, and parents learn about the living world and find out why biology is so interesting that people choose to make a living working in this field. The site includes activities, stories, images, podcasts, puzzles, and word games for different educational levels.
311	Association for Middle Level Education (AMLE)	The AMLE collection focuses on STEM curricula, middle grade pedagogy and assessment, young adolescent development, leadership, and professional development. The collection has resources for educators, classroom teachers, and principals to develop more effective schools.
25	Atmospheric Visualization Collection	The Atmospheric Visualization Collection (AVC) is intended to enhance physical science education and research through visualization of atmospheric data. This collection includes an archive of atmospheric data images and educational material based on these images. By utilizing collaborative digital library tools, a growing user community assists in the development of this collection.
41	Atomic Archive	This site explores the science, history, and consequences of the invention of the atomic bomb. It offers information about the events and decisions that led to the development of the bomb and the events and decisions that followed, from Hiroshima and Nagasaki to today's post–Cold War era. The site explains basic atomic physics, nuclear fission, and nuclear fusion. It also explores the effects of nuclear weapons and ponders several "what-if" scenarios. The history section tells the stories of the first nuclear reactor and the first nuclear test in New Mexico's desert. A Resource Library includes historical documents and biographies of nuclear pioneers, including J. Robert Oppenheimer, Albert Einstein, Edward Teller, Enrico Fermi, Hans Bethe. The site offers educators teaching aids such as interactive maps, animations, a timeline of the nuclear age, and a glossary of terms. The Nuclear News section offers topical summaries of current events pertaining to nuclear issues.

(continued)

Number of Records	Title	Description
480	Beyond Penguins and Polar Bears	An online magazine for K–5 teachers, this collection provides resources that help elementary educators teach hands-on science, integrate literacy and science, and incorporate polar science topics into existing curriculums.
71	*Beyond Weather and the Water Cycle*	*Beyond Weather and the Water Cycle* is an online professional development magazine that focuses on preparing elementary teachers to teach climate science concepts, and to integrate inquiry-based science and literacy instruction. Structured around the seven essential principles of climate literacy and using an Earth-systems approach, the instructional and professional resources provided can improve elementary teacher understanding of climate science and change. By using this site teachers can more effectively prepare even the youngest students to study and shape climate policy in the future.
151	Biological Sciences Gateways and Resources	The Biological Sciences Gateways and Resources collection is composed of Web portals, websites, and individual digital resources in many areas of the biological and life sciences, including agriculture, botany, ecology, genetics, microbiology, natural history, marine biology, zoology, and others. The collection includes educational materials for life science educators and learners, resources intended for the general public, and materials aimed at biological sciences research communities.
19277	BiosciEdNet (BEN): Digital Library Portal for Teaching and Learning in the Biological Sciences	BiosciEdNet (BEN) is a catalyst for biology educators to improve their teaching through resources, collaboration, and network building. It also helps participating biology research-based and education-based organizations build collaborations in terms of pedagogy, authentic assessment, multidisciplinary resources, and development of their individual digital-library collections. Materials in the digital library are designed primarily for undergraduate biology educators, including those who prepare K–12 faculty members. The BEN Collaborative is produced by the American Association for the Advancement of Science (AAAS).
10	Black Box Software Testing	The Black Box Software Testing Collection provides instructional materials (i.e., lectures, slides, videos) to teach black box software testing. Materials in the collection are organized into self-contained sections that focus on foundations of software testing and specific, well-known software-testing techniques.

91	Bridge-NOAA Collection	The Bridge-NOAA Collection is a selection of exemplary resources that have been reviewed by educators and found to be well-suited for educational purposes. The collection also emphasizes professional-development opportunities for teachers. It has a strong focus on research data and its use in teaching.
557	Bridge: Sea Grant Ocean Sciences Resources Center	The Bridge: Sea Grant Ocean Sciences Resources Center provides access to ocean sciences educational materials. The collection also includes links to information about professional-development opportunities for teachers. There is a strong focus on research data and its use in teaching. The collection provides accurate and useful information on global, national, and regional ocean science topics, and gives researchers a contact point for educational outreach.
645	CLEAN Review Teaching Tips	The CLEAN (Climate Literacy and Energy Awareness Network) pathway provides a collection of teaching tips that facilitate students, teachers, and citizens in becoming climate literate and informed about climate and energy science.
635	CLEAN: Climate Literacy and Energy Awareness Network	The CLEAN collection supports and provides outreach to these developing communities in grades 6 through undergraduate, Climate and energy topics include climate system, causes of climate change, measuring and modeling climate, impacts of climate change, human responses to climate change, and energy use. Resources are reviewed for scientific accuracy and pedagogic relevancy.
196	COMET Program Collection	The COMET Program Collection and its MetEd (Meteorology Education and Training) collection provide educational and training resources. Included are images, tutorials, visualizations, meteorological data, and learning materials on climate, icing, convective weather, fog and low stratus, hydrology, satellite meteorology, numerical weather prediction, winter weather, hurricanes, and other mesoscale meteorology topics.
1850	CSERD: Computational Science Education Reference Desk	The Computational Science Education Reference Desk (CSERD) features resources to help students learn about computational science and to help teachers incorporate it into the classroom. The Resources section of the CSERD site provides a permanent collection of materials developed especially for CSERD, including models (pieces of scientific software), activities (lessons or lesson plans that use models), tutorials (short courses designed to teach a specific topic), applications, algorithms, and architectures.

(continued)

Number of Records	Title	Description
136	CTE Online	The CTE (Career and Technical Education) Online site offers mainly math resources aligned to the mathematics Common Core educational standards.
449	Case Study Collection: National Center for Case Study Teaching in Science	The Case Study Collection makes science relevant by presenting contemporary science problems about issues that students encounter in real life. The case studies in the collection are created by science and engineering faculty, and facilitate a powerful pedagogical technique for teaching scientific concepts and content, while also advancing student process skills and critical thinking. The cases are published after undergoing peer review and revision, and all cases have teaching notes—including classroom management and assessment strategies with answer keys—and printable student materials.
95	Center for Advanced Automotive Technology	The Center for Advanced Automotive Technology (CAAT) houses a comprehensive, up-to-date educational resource library in the fields of automotive engineering and technology.
58	Centers for Ocean Sciences Education Excellence (COSEE)	The Centers for Ocean Sciences Education Excellence (COSEE) website provides access to ocean sciences educational materials with accurate and useful information on global, national, and regional ocean science topics, and provides researchers with a contact point for educational outreach.
12	Changing Planet	This video collection uses interviews, maps, simulations, and real-world film footage to illustrate how climate change influences the environments around us—from lakes, oceans, and glaciers to permafrost, ice, and crops. Each video has a related free lesson plan from the National Earth Science Teachers Association.
21	ChemCases: General Chemistry Case Studies	ChemCases offers curriculum supplements appropriate for teaching the second semester of an undergraduate general chemistry course. The supplements are twelve case studies examining the chemistry of products that the general public often encounters, such as sports drinks, refrigerants, automotive fuels, and alcoholic beverages. Each case study features a number of the basic principles covered in a traditional general chemistry course. The concepts are used to explore the decisions that influenced the development of successful consumer, agricultural, and pharmaceutical products. ChemCases explains the benign and explores the controversial, moving the science of chemistry into the mainstream of decision making.

112	ChemTeacher	ChemTeacher compiles resources such as articles, worksheets, activities, demonstrations, and videos for use by secondary school teachers and students. Resources are linked to common chemistry topics and are searchable by science standards.
1185	Chemical Education Digital Library (ChemEdDL)	The ChemEd Digital Library provides exemplary resources, tools, and online services to aid in teaching and learning chemistry. Major resources center on the periodic table and properties of the elements, molecular and solid-state structures, videos showing chemical reactions, questions for homework and quizzes, virtual laboratories, and Wiki-based textbooks. Major services include a course-management system (Moodle) into which resources are easily added, a tool for organizing Wiki-textbooks into course units, and a series of high-school chemistry lesson plans incorporating online resources.
38	Chemistry Gateways and Resources	The Chemistry Gateways and Resources collection is composed of chemistry-related Web portals, websites, and individual digital resources pertaining to many areas of the discipline, such as general chemistry, organic and inorganic chemistry, and physical chemistry.
1205	Choosing and Using DLESE (Digital Library for Earth System Education)	The Choosing and Using DLESE highlights resources from DLESE (Digital Library for Earth System Education) that have some associated pedagogical content knowledge. This knowledge can include formal and informal reviews, annotations, educational standards (national, state, and local), comments, teaching tips (includes using resources with special-needs audiences), and other quantitative evaluation information.
19	Citizen Science	The Citizen Science collection contains links to various Citizen Science projects that teachers and parents can use to engage their students in real-world data collection and analysis.
182	ComPADRE Classroom-Ready Resources	The ComPADRE Classroom-Ready Resources collection consists of physics learning resources deemed by editors to be of the very highest quality. The resources also meet strict criteria for inclusion: Representative of evidence-based best practices; accurate in content; accessible; easy to implement in the classroom; pedagogically appropriate; and aligned to national standards. The Classroom-Ready Collection particularly emphasizes multimedia learning objects, resources that include assessments and content support, and materials that promote active learning experiences.

(continued)

Number of Records	Title	Description
7387	ComPADRE: Resources for Physics and Astronomy Education	ComPADRE is composed of communities of teachers and students in physics and astronomy and Web-based collections of resources that support their needs. The communities supported by Com-PADRE are those which can benefit from the sharing of materials, information, and experiences in a Web environment. Example communities include teachers of specific physics or astronomy courses, undergraduate physics and astronomy student societies, and teachers addressing specific grade levels (such as high-school or middle-school teachers). Resources included in the collections are chosen to enhance the teaching and learning experience, and include multimedia learning objects, lesson plans, tutorials, laboratories, and other student activities, plus discussion forums on the use of these materials. The different collections are organized under the ComPADRE umbrella, which provides a central database (the Physical Sciences Resource Center), technical support, support for collection editors and community leaders, and the means to coordinate efforts across the communities.
29	Computer Science and Information Technology Gateways and Resources	The Computer Science and Information Technology Gateways and Resources collection is composed of Web portals, websites, and resources in many areas. The collection includes algorithms and data structures, operating systems and programming languages, software engineering, artificial intelligence, information science, digital-library technologies, and others.
84	Concord Consortium Collection	The Concord Consortium Collection includes free science, engineering, and mathematics activities for grades 3 through 14. It integrates probes and models including the award-winning Molecular Workbench.
5	Curricular Resource Library (cURL): Earth and Environmental Sciences	The cURL Earth and Environmental Sciences collection provides access to educational materials emphasizing the origin, evolution, and current state of the Earth. The collection targets undergraduate students and offers access to information about solid-earth geological processes, surficial processes, geochemistry, ecology, and aquatic sciences.
50	Digital Library for Earth System Education (DLESE) Collections	The Digital Library for Earth System Education (DLESE) Collections showcases the different collections within the Digital Library for Earth System Education (DLESE).

5756	Digital Library for Earth System Education (DLESE) Community Collection	The mission of the Digital Library for Earth System Education is to improve the quality, quantity, and efficiency of teaching and learning about the Earth System, by developing, managing, and providing access to high-quality educational resources and supporting services through a community-based, distributed digital library. The collection includes Earth data sets and imagery, and the tools and interfaces that enable their effective use.
75	Demos with Positive Impact	Demos with Positive Impact collection features short materials that can be used in classroom presentations. The demos use a range of technology from animated gifs to java applets.
123	Developmental Mathematics Collection (DMC)	The Developmental Mathematics Collection (DMC) contains resources for community college educators teaching basic arithmetic through intermediate algebra. Resources include student activities, topic teaching plans, innovative curricula and course sequences, as well as research syntheses on pedagogy and learning.
258	Digital Water Education Library (DWEL)	The Digital Water Education Library (DWEL) collection offers high-quality K–12 and informal-education digital resources related to the science, policy, and economics of water. The collection is designed to facilitate learning about all aspects of water in the Earth System.
342	DragonflyTV	DragonflyTV is an Emmy Award–winning PBS Kids science show, featuring ordinary kids conducting extraordinary inquiry-based investigations in real-world contexts. DragonflyTV features investigations, scientist profiles, hands-on science activities, and Flash-based games.
49	Earth Exploration Toolbook (EET)	The Earth Exploration Toolbook (EET) is a collection of step-by-step examples of the use of Earth System science resources in an educational context. The resources include data sets, analysis tools, visualization tools, and other educational products. Each chapter features one specific resource.
43	Earth System Science Informal Education Network (ESSIEN)	The Earth System Science Informal Education Network (ESSIEN) is a collection is designed for museum professionals (i.e., educators, exhibits designers, developers) as a resource of ideas, tools, traveling exhibits, and online materials. The resources are Web portals to organizations providing substantial informal Earth System science education. They describe educational programming, resources, and exhibits that are pertinent to an informal educator.

(continued)

Number of Records	Title	Description
5	EarthLabs	EarthLabs is a collection of challenging, lab-based high school Earth science teacher's guides, pedagogical guidance, assessments, and curriculum units. Each integrates text, hands-on activities, interactive visualizations, video, authentic science data, and data visualization and analysis tools.
115	Earthquake Education Environment (E3)	The Earthquake Education Environment (E3) collection supports high-quality K–12 and undergraduate education by providing up-to-date earthquake information, authoritative technical sources, and educational resources for the classroom.
66	Engineering and Technology Gateways and Resources	The Engineering and Technology Gateways and Resources collection is composed of Web portals, websites, and resources in many areas of engineering and technology. Areas covered include mechanical, civil, chemical, electrical, industrial, environmental, and nuclear engineering; biotechnology and nanotechnology; and chemical, environmental, manufacturing, and process technologies.
53	Environmental Science Activities for the 21st Century	The Environmental Science Activities for the 21st Century collection provides multi-week activity modules centered on major topics in environmental science. The modules are designed to supplement environmental science courses with existing laboratory components or to provide course activities for traditional and online courses that lack a laboratory component. The activities hybridize online and wet-lab exercises to take advantage of both formats and utilize existing high-quality materials available on the Internet. Modules cover the atmosphere, basic science, biogeochemical cycles, energy, fossil fuels, nuclear energy, ozone, renewable energy, and water.
351	Fun Works . . . for Careers You Never Knew Existed	The Fun Works (Education Development Center, Inc.) is a digital library of career exploration resources for youths aged 11 to 15. The Fun Works provides "real-world" experiences and uses the current interests and passions of younger learners—such as music and sports—to help them explore exciting careers in science, technology, engineering, and mathematics (STEM), and other areas.
131	GLOBE Teacher's Guide	The Global Learning and Observations to Benefit the Environment (GLOBE) collection mainly is composed of teachers' guides, field guides, and classroom activities that engage teachers and students in measuring protocols of different environmental variables such as temperature, optical thickness, cloud cover, ozone, precipitation, and water vapor.

94	General Science and STEM Gateways and Resources	The General Science and STEM Gateways and Resources collection is composed of Web portals, websites, and individual digital resources. The collection includes portals and sites offering material on three or more scientific disciplines or on the entire STEM spectrum. It also offers substantial material devoted to the nature of science and scientific method. Also included are individual resources focusing on the nature of science and scientific method.
109	Geosciences Gateways and Resources	The Geosciences Gateways and Resources collection is composed of Web portals, websites, and individual digital resources from many areas of the geosciences. It includes materials on atmospheric sciences, environmental sciences, geology, geophysics, hydrology, oceanography, physical geography, soil science, and other Earth-science subjects.
15	Health Sciences Gateways and Resources	The Health Sciences Gateways and Resources collection is composed of Web portals, websites, and individual digital resources from many areas of the health sciences. It includes materials on aging, biostatistics, body systems and senses, consumer health, diseases, environmental health, epidemiology, human sexuality, and nutrition.
12	Hiroshima and Nagasaki Remembered	This website provides an easy-to-use collection of resources to help students, educators, and the general public better understand Hiroshima and Nagasaki. The website offers original texts, eyewitness accounts, historical documents, rare photographs, videos, and full-color maps.
24	History of Science and Technology Gateways and Resources	The History of Science and Technology Gateways and Resources collection is composed of Web portals, websites, and individual digital resources devoted to many eras of the history of science and the history of technology.
952	Illustrative Mathematics	Illustrative Mathematics provides guidance to states, assessment consortia, testing companies, and curriculum developers by illustrating the range and types of mathematical work that students experience in a faithful implementation of the Common Core State Standards, and by publishing other tools that support implementation of the standards.
24,754	Internet Scout Project	The Internet Scout Report evaluates and annotates high-quality online resources—particularly those of value to the education community. Each resource is selected, researched, and annotated by a team of professional librarians and subject-matter experts, who evaluate sites on the basis of their content, authority, upkeep, presentation, availability, and cost.

(continued)

Number of Records	Title	Description
37	Jonathan Bird's Blue World	Jonathan Bird's Blue World collection is based on a public television science adventure series. It offers science curriculum–based videos, lesson plans, and activities. It can be searched by topic, NSES, and geography. The materials included illustrate topics such as sound, osmosis, and pH and include videos of sperm whales, mangroves, and coral reefs.
43	Key Concepts in Algebra	The Key Concepts in Algebra collection provides quick and easy access to high-quality high school algebra resources.
64	Key Concepts in Biology	The Key Concepts in Biology collection provides quick and easy access to high-quality high school biology resources. This curriculum highlights eight key concepts in six units of study: Evolution; Homeostasis; Energy; Matter and Organization; Reproduction and Inheritance in Living Systems; Growth; Development and Differentiation; and Ecology.
92	MY NASA DATA	The MY NASA DATA collection showcases NASA Earth-science data through lesson plans, data micro sets, computer tools, data information pages, and a science glossary. Resources cover clouds, aerosols, the radiation budget, and tropospheric chemistry. The collection emphasizes data and the tools used to analyze it.
6	Math Forum Collection	The Math Forum Collection features a K–12 math expert service (Ask Dr. Math), a database of math sites and math tools, online resources for teaching and learning math, a discussion forum, and information on professional-development events and programs. Most items are available by subscription, but some resources are available with free registration or by direct link.
20	Math Images	The Math Images project is a collection of images related to mathematics, together with discussions of the math behind the images. Users are encouraged to contribute information, new pages, and questions, and to share ideas and interact. The math images are meant to inspire a greater interest in mathematics.
63	Mathematics Gateways and Resources	The Mathematics Gateways and Resources collection is composed of K–graduate school level mathematics-related Web portals, websites, and individual digital resources. The collection includes many areas of the discipline, such as algebra, applied math, arithmetic, calculus, functions, geometry, measurement, number sense, probability, and statistics.

1771	Mathlanding: Elementary Mathematics Pathway	The Mathlanding Pathway offers high-quality digital mathematics content and contextualized resources, enabling educators to easily incorporate the materials into effective instructional practice. This NSDL Pathway is provided by Maryland Public Television (MPT), the Math Forum at Drexel University, and the International Society for Technology in Education (ISTE) to foster excellence in elementary mathematics education, and is targeted to support elementary classroom teachers and specialists, coaches, supervisors, educators involved in teacher preparation, and parents.
448	Microbial Life Educational Resources (MLER)	Microbial Life Educational Resources aims to provide a contemporary and expanding collection of resources of expert information about the ecology, diversity, and evolution of microorganisms built around themes, primarily microbial life in extreme environments and microbial life in oceans.
2623	Middle School Portal: Math and Science Pathways (MSP2)	The Middle School Portal: Math and Science Pathways supports middle grades educators with high-quality, standards-based resources, and promotes collaboration and knowledge-sharing among its users. The MSP2 employs social networking and digital tools to foster dynamic experiences that promote creation, modification, and sharing of resources; facilitates professional development; and supports the integration of technology into practice.
56	Minds-On Activities for Teaching Biology	The Minds-On Activities include discussion activities, Web-based activities, experiments, and simulation activities to foster student understanding of important concepts in the life sciences. Topics covered include biological molecules, membranes and osmosis, cellular respiration and photosynthesis, cell structure and function, cell division, genetics, molecular biology, evolution, diversity, human physiology and health, and design and interpretation of experiments.
459	NASA Earth and Space Science Education Collection	The NASA Earth and Space Science Education Collection provides teachers and students with a wide variety of curriculum enhancement materials geared toward Earth science classroom use.
494	NASA Earth and Space Science Reviewed Collection	The NASA Earth and Space Science Reviewed Collection provides educators and students with a direct line of access to quality products reviewed using the NASA product review. This is based on scientific accuracy, educational value, documentation, ease of use, the power to engage or motivate students, their robustness/sustainability as a digital resource, and the ability to foster mastery of significant understandings or skills.

(continued)

Number of Records	Title	Description
2029	NASA Wavelength	NASA Wavelength is a digital collection of Earth and space science resources for educators of all levels—elementary, college, and out-of-school programs. These resources—developed through funding of the NASA Science Mission Directorate (SMD)—have undergone a peer-review process through which educators and scientists ensure that the content is accurate and useful in an educational setting.
137	NSDL Bilingual Collection	The NSDL Bilingual Collection makes K–12 math and science resources available to teachers of students who are not proficient in English. The majority of the non-English-language resources are in Spanish, but there also are many resources available in Portuguese, French, German, and Italian.
26	NSDL English Language Arts	The NSDL English Language Arts collection provides quick and easy access to high-quality math resources that have been related to the English Language Arts Science and Technical Standards.
388	NSDL Math Common Core	The NSDL Math Common Core collection provides quick and easy access to high-quality math resources that have been related to one or more standard statements within the Math Common Core.
167	NSDL Science Refreshers	NSDL Science Refreshers provide quick and easy access to high-quality science content from trusted providers. Materials are selected and organized by grade level and subject area to enhance content knowledge.
9	NSDL Web Seminars	The National Science Digital Library (NSDL) collaborated with NSTA to develop seminars that are focused on a variety of science topics and target K–12 grade educators.
123	National Curve Bank	The National Curve Bank displays representations of two- and three-dimensional curves. Geometrical, algebraic, and historical aspects of curves are included. Educators and students have access to animations, interactions, java applets, Mathematica code, and more. Users may submit curves.
133	National Science Foundation (NSF) Special Reports and Videos	The NSF Special Reports and Videos collection features scientific work being performed using NSF funding. Topics include weather, evolution, mathematics, visualization, technology, polar, infectious disease, robotics, wild animals, earthquake engineering, cyberinfrastructure, tsunami, the arctic, and climates.

6242	National Science Teachers Association (NSTA) Learning Center	The NSTA Learning Center offers print and online resources for science teachers, including a wealth of journal articles, books, book chapters, and electronic professional-development resources, such as SciGuides, SciPacks, and Web seminars. The NSTA Learning Center content covers many important educational topics, such as achievement, assessment of students, classroom management, curriculum, inquiry learning, instructional materials, learning theory, integrating technology, professional development, student populations, teacher content knowledge, teacher preparation, and teacher strategies.
68	New York State Earth Science Instructional Collection (NYSESIC)	The NYSESIC is a thematic collection focusing on instructional materials that support teaching and learning in relation to the New York Earth Science Regents exam. The topics include solid Earth forms and processes, atmospheric composition and dynamics, forms and mechanics of water, bodies and mechanics in space, Earth history, and Earth models.
2750	On the Cutting Edge: Professional Development for Geoscience Faculty and Bibliographies	The Cutting Edge collection is a set of thematic strands on pedagogical and content topics including biocomplexity, early-career faculty development, petrology, and designing effective courses in the geosciences. Resources include instructional materials, activities, data sets, interfaces and tools, pedagogical resources, course development and management resources, assessment instruments, and primary literature.
36	Online Psychology Laboratory (OPL)	The Online Psychology Laboratory consists of highly interactive, Web-deliverable psychology experiments and demonstrations; a cumulative data archive from which students can retrieve data sets for analysis; and user-controlled data extraction and analysis tools designed for the diverse needs of end users.
299	PBS Learning Media Common Core Collection	This collection provides a selection of 300 resources drawn from PBS Learning Media. Each was chosen because it represents an approach to using digital media to support the Common Core State Standards for English Language Arts and Literacy in Science and Technical Subjects, the Common Core State Standards for Mathematics, or the approaches to science education discussed in the Framework for K–12 Science Education.
2106	PBS Learning Media: Multimedia Resources for the Classroom and Professional Development	PBS Learning Media is a multimedia library for K–12 science educators. It includes content from *NOVA*, *A Science Odyssey*, *Evolution*, and other programs. Each classroom resource is correlated to state and national science standards. The professional-development content includes video of teachers modeling best practices in their classroom instruction; interviews with educators reflecting on effective classroom strategies; and online development courses for elementary science educators.

(continued)

Number of Records	Title	Description
240	PRISMS: Phenomena and Representations for the Instruction of Science in Middle School	PRISMS: Phenomena and Representations for the Instruction of Science in Middle School provides annotated reviews describing a resource's phenomenon or representation content alignment and quality of instructional support. It focuses on resources useful to science instruction in middle school. Resources are evaluated for how well they support learning goals in Science for All Americans, Benchmarks for Science Literacy, and the National Science Education Standards.
123	Paleontological Research Institution (PRI)—Museum of the Earth	The Paleontological Research Institution is a natural history museum that has exhibits and programs which cover the entire spectrum of the history of the Earth and its life, with a particular focus on the Northeastern United States.
1419	Pedagogy in Action	The Pedagogy in Action collection provides educator-focused introductions to a range of teaching methods that promote engaged learning. It combines "what," "why," and "how" information about the pedagogies with descriptions of real-world teaching activities that exemplify each method.
128	PhET Interactive Simulations	The PhET Interactive Simulations include fun, interactive, research-based simulations of physical phenomena from biology, math, physics, earth science, and chemistry. The PhET simulations animate what is invisible to the naked eye by using graphics and intuitive controls such as click-and-drag manipulation, sliders, and radio buttons. The simulations also offer measurement instruments including rulers, stop-watches, voltmeters, and thermometers to illustrate cause-and-effect relationships as well as multiple linked representations (e.g., motion of the objects, graphs, number readouts.).
54	Physics Gateways and Resources	The Physics Gateways and Resources collection is composed of physics-related Web portals, web-sites, and individual digital resources in many areas of the discipline, including electromagnetism, classical mechanics, optics, oscillations and waves, quantum mechanics, and thermodynamics.
281	Plant and Soil Sciences eLibrary	The Plant and Soil Sciences eLibrary is a collection of interactive animations, eLessons, video clips, and quizzes on plant genetics, biotechnology, soil science, and weed science. Its target audiences are high school students and beyond.

10	This site helps new and existing users of Rapid Prototyping (RP) develop a better understanding of the technology. Materials include guidance in the development of distance learning materials, technology transfer approaches, marketing materials, understanding of the incorporation of RP in the manufacturing design process, and maintenance procedures for RP equipment.
Rapid Prototyping Instructional Delivery Support	
558	The Reciprocal Net is a digital collection of molecular structures in crystallography and chemistry with innovative visualizing tools to view structural details of substances. For each molecular structure the chemical formula and an explanation is given. The website also has other reference information, and some demonstrations and learning modules.
Reciprocal Net: A Distributed Crystallography Network for Researchers, Students, and the General Public	
246	SMARTR provides students and teachers with games, simulations, activities, and career information in mathematics and the sciences. Science topics include earthquakes, chemistry, weather, rocks, the solar system, the body, genetics, and energy. Mathematics topics covered include ratios, probability, measurement, graphing, 3D geometry, equations, and statistics.
SMARTR: Virtual Learning Experiences for Youth	
3316	The SMILE (Science and Math Informal Learning Educators) Pathway is for informal educators seeking high-quality STEM activities across multiple disciplines and contributing institutions.
Science and Math Informal Learning Educators (SMILE) Pathway: Science and Math Activities in One Search	
48	The STEM (Science, Technology, Engineering, and Mathematics) Education and Educational Technology Gateways and Resources collection is composed of Web portals, websites, and individual digital resources devoted to educational theory and practice. It includes ideas and practices in the teaching of science, technology, engineering, and mathematics, as well as resources and gateways that focus on the uses of technology in the classroom.
STEM Education and Educational Technology Gateways and Resources	

(continued)

Number of Records	Title	Description
10	Science Friday	Science Friday is a trusted source for news and entertaining stories about science. In addition to the radio program, Science Friday produces engaging educational resources, award-winning digital videos, and original Web content covering everything from octopus camouflage to cooking on Mars. SciFri is "brain fun for curious people."
189	Science for Kids	The ACS collection Science for Kids mainly presents chemistry and physics concepts at a level that kids in grades K through 8 can understand. Also included are interviews with practicing chemists who teach students about various career options that use chemistry. Many resources are available in Spanish.
10	Science of NFL Football	NBC Learn—with the NSF and the NFL—unravels the science behind professional football. Featuring footage from games and practice sessions, and contributions from football players and scientists, the series presents students with examples drawn from the NFL. It addresses concepts such as nutrition, kinematics, torque, vectors, Newton's Laws, and projectile motion. Each video has related lesson plans that include classroom and extended activities.
10	Science of NHL Hockey	NBC Learn and NBC Sports—in partnership with the NSF and the NHL—explore the science and math behind professional hockey. Featuring game footage and contributions from NHL players and scientists, the 10-part series uses hockey to demonstrate such key concepts as Newton's Law, kinematics, collisions, projectile motion, vectors, and basic geometry. Each video has related lesson plans that include classroom and extended activities.
43	Science of Winter	Science of Winter is a collection of activities, lessons, interactives, images, and other content illustrating or demonstrating scientific aspects of winter weather, conditions, processes, or phenomena. It is appropriate for middle school, informal education, and general audiences.
2185	Scientific Visualization Studio	The NASA Scientific Visualization Studio collection contains visualizations of geophysical phenomena produced from satellite data or from computer simulations using satellite data. The visualizations show physical phenomena that occur on Earth, other planets, and on the sun. The visualizations focus on natural events such as hurricanes, fires, and floods; virtual zooms and fly-bys of cities and interesting geographic areas of Earth and Mars; and daily, seasonal, annual, or decadal variations of snow, sea ice, ozone, sea surface temperature, aerosols, land cover, and ocean productivity.

16	Simplified Image Management and Processing Learning Environment for Science (SIMPLE Science)	The Simplified Image Management and Processing Learning Environment for Science (SIMPLE Science) collection emphasizes image processing and analysis techniques that meet educational standards. The collection features tutorials that guide students through case studies replicating research conducted by leading imaging scientists, and explains key concepts in imaging science. The primary Earth science areas used in the case studies are snow and ice, hurricanes, ozone holes, and planet size.
27	Social Sciences Gateways and Resources	The Social Sciences Gateways and Resources collection is composed of Web portals, websites, and individual digital resources devoted to the interplay of science and the social realm, as well as social-science materials that draw heavily upon—or are closely related to—the life sciences, physical sciences, mathematics, and technology: It includes, for example, archaeology, physical anthropology, economics, human geography, linguistics, and psychology.
51	Space Sciences Gateways and Resources	The Space Sciences Gateways and Resources collection is composed of Web portals, websites, and individual digital resources in many areas pertinent to the study of space. It includes materials on astrochemistry, astrophysics, cosmology, the solar system, extrasolar planets, amateur astronomy, information about observatories and space exploration, and many other subjects.
137	TRUST Academy Online (TAO)	TRUST Academy Online (TAO) Project Profiles share the stories of individual TRUST cybersecurity projects and provide access to related resources. The TAO Courseware Profiles include sets of learning materials developed by TRUST investigators, institutions, and partners.
451	Teach the Earth	The Teach the Earth collection from the Science Education Resource Center (SERC) collection spans middle school through graduate level education with a special emphasis on undergraduate education. It includes thematic foci such as teaching quantitative skills, integrating current geoscience research into education, preparing K–12 earth science teachers, and teaching with data.
1404	TeachEngineering: Resources for K–12	The TeachEngineering digital library provides teacher-tested, standards-based engineering content for K–12 teachers to use in science and math classrooms. Engineering lessons connect real-world experiences with curricular content already taught in K–12 classrooms.

(continued)

Number of Records	Title	Description
24	TeachSpatial	The TeachSpatial collection assembles digital teaching resources relevant to spatial cognition, spatial learning, and spatial literacy across multiple STEM disciplines for middle school, high school, and undergraduate learners. Common topics include physical geography, GIS (Geographic Information Systems), and map-reading skills (e.g., population demographics, geographic coordinates).
559	TeachingWithData. org	TeachingWithData.org provides a portal to materials that help faculty integrate quantitative analysis within social science courses.
6	The GLOBE Collection	The Global Learning and Observations to Benefit the Environment (GLOBE) collection features teaching resources created by NASA, NOAA, and NSF Earth System Science Projects (ESSPs).
55	Virtual Laboratories in Probability and Statistics	Virtual Laboratories in Probability and Statistics provides free, high-quality, interactive, Web-based resources for students and teachers of probability and statistics, including expository text, applets, data sets, biographical sketches, and an object library.
46	Visionlearning	Visionlearning provides peer-reviewed teaching modules in chemistry, biology, earth science, and other disciplines within a fully customizable online classroom management system.
23	Web Adventures: Explore Science One Game at a Time	Web Adventures offers a series of problem-based learning adventure games that engage players in various science-related roles and hands-on activities such as quizzes, activities, and mission logs. The MedMyst series also offers a magazine for helping students reinforce reading and writing skills.
81	Wisconsin Fast Plants Activity and Resource Library	Wisconsin Fast Plants Activity and Resource Library is a growing collection of educational materials developed over more than 25 years (and continuing) for science educators at all levels and science researchers who support learning science concepts using the model organism, Rapid Cycling Brassica rapa.
11	Wolfram Research	The Wolfram Research collection includes access to the comprehensive and interactive mathematics encyclopedias of MathWorld and the Wolfram Functions Site.

Appendix C

K–12 STEM OER
Video Collections

Title	URL	Description
American Memory	http://memory.loc.gov/ammem/browse/ListSome.php?format=Motion+Picture	This collection provides a wide range of historically significant materials in a variety of formats. The video clips are available via streaming media and/or in mpeg (downloadable) format.
Archive.org	http://www.archive.org/details/movies	The Internet Archive includes texts, audio, moving images, and software as well as archived Web pages in its collections, and provides specialized services for adaptive reading and information access for the blind and other persons with disabilities.
ARKive	http://arkive.org	This collection of videos and photographs is based on the understanding that wildlife imagery is "an emotive and effective means of building environmental awareness and engagement." Users can search the collection by wildlife species or by image format.
Explo.tv	http://www.exploratorium.edu/webcasts/archive.php?cmd=browse&presentation_type=all	Explo.tv is part of the Exploratorium's online science museum presence. Videos can be searched by media type, content format, category, and keyword.
Harvard-Smithsonian Center for Astrophysics Digital Video Library	http://www.hsdvl.org/viewall.php	This video collection features "clinical interviews of student ideas; demonstrations of phenomena; case studies of instruction or research; and interviews with experts." Videos can be searched in a variety of ways, including the use of AAAS (American Association for the Advancement of Science) Benchmarks, the use of state standards, the use of instructional criteria, and the use of a graphical "strand map."
Instant Replay	http://www.knowitall.org/InstantReplay/	This small collection includes freely available streaming videos on a wide variety of subjects, ranging from school reform plans to the Tuskegee Airmen. One of its most extensive collections is "Zoo Minutes," which contains one-minute video clips of different animals.
InTime	http://www.intime.uni.edu/	InTime enables educators to watch online video vignettes of Pre-K through Grade 12 teachers (teaching various subjects) who integrate technology into their classrooms using numerous teaching strategies.

Khan Academy	http://www.khanacademy.org/	Offers a library of more than 2,700 videos, covering everything from arithmetic to physics, finance, and history, and including 276 practice exercises.
NASA for Educators / NASA for Students	http://www.nasa.gov	NASA provides Web-native video clips and clips drawn from its published DVDs along with learning support for teachers and students.
National Geographic Video	http://video.nationalgeographic.com/video/	Videos can be searched within categories. For each video, the site provides links to related National Geographic materials located elsewhere on the website. In addition to subject-specific categories, the site also offers featured videos, most-watched videos, videos in the news, and a means for users to submit their own videos to "Everyday Explorers."
NOVA and NOVA scienceNOW	http://www.pbs.org/wgbh/nova/teachers/video/	"NOVA is the highest rated science series on television and the most watched documentary series on public television." This site enables users to view NOVA programs in their entirety and to view individual segments of NOVA scienceNOW episodes.
Open Vault	http://openvault.wgbh.org/	Open Vault provides free online access to aspects of the WGBH Media Library and Archives' collection of historically important content produced by public television station WGBH. The site contains video clips from a wide variety of television series and users can search by keyword, series, person, or subject.
Perspectives	http://www.cpalms.org/cpalms/perspectives.aspx	The CPALMS Perspectives initiative provides standards-aligned brief video resources highlighting experiences and thoughts regarding math and science from experts, teachers, professionals, and skilled enthusiasts.
ResearchChannel	http://www.youtube.com/ResearchChannel	ResearchChannel is a consortium of research universities and corporate research divisions dedicated to broadening the access to and appreciation of individual and collective activities, ideas, and opportunities in basic and applied research. Streaming videos can be searched by keyword, or browsed by title, institution, subject, or new releases.

(continued)

Title	URL	Description
Schoolyard Films	http://schoolyardfilms.org/	The mission of Schoolyard Films is to educate students about the natural world and the challenges it faces.
Thinkport	http://www.thinkport.org/Classroom/onlineclips.tp	This collection provides users with a wide range of historically significant materials in a variety of formats. The video clips are available via streaming media and/or in mpeg (downloadable) format.
WatchKnowLearn	http://watchknowlearn.org	WatchKnowLearn has indexed more than 20,000 educational videos, placing them into a directory of more than 3,000 categories. Video titles, descriptions, age level information, and ratings are all edited for usefulness.
Wide Angle	http://www.pbs.org/wnet/wideangle/category/video/watch-full-episodes/	The programs consist of interviews with foreign policy experts, journalists, politicians, and world leaders who provide context and critical perspective on how global issues connect to American concerns and U.S. foreign policy. Programs are divided into "chapters" that can be viewed individually.

References

Achieve, Inc. 2011. "Rubrics for Evaluating Open Education Resource (OER) Objects." Last modified November 18, 2011. http://www.achieve.org/files/AchieveOERRubrics.pdf.

Achieve, Inc. 2013. "Appendix F–Science and Engineering Practices in the NGSS." Accessed June 2, 2014. http://www.nextgenscience.org/sites/ngss/files/Appendix F Science and Engineering Practices in the NGSS-FINAL 060513.pdf.

Achieve, Inc. 2014. "Lead State Partners." Accessed June 2, 2014. http://www.nextgenscience.org/lead-state-partners.

American Association for the Advancement of Science [AAAS]. 1990. Accessed August 12, 2014. "Chapter 13: Effective Learning and Teaching." http://www.project2061.org/publications/sfaa/online/chap13.htm.

American Association of School Librarians [AASL]. 2009a. *Empowering Learners: Guidelines for School Library Media Programs.* Chicago, IL: American Library Association.

American Association of School Librarians [AASL]. 2009b. *Standards for the 21st Century Learner in Action.* Chicago, IL: American Library Association.

American Association of School Librarians [AASL]. 2011. "School Libraries Count! National Longitudinal Survey of School Library Programs." Accessed September 1, 2011. http://www.ala.org/aasl/sites/ala.org.aasl/files/content/researchandstatistics/slcsurvey/2011/AASL-SLC-2011-FINALweb.pdf.

American Association of School Librarians [AASL], and Association for Educational Communications and Technology [AECT]. 1998. *Information Power: Building Partnerships for Learning.* Chicago, IL: American Library Association.

Aptaker, R. 2013. "Destiny as a One-Stop Shop Part 2." Last modified September 13, 2013. http://www.follettsoftware.com/LibraryConnections/post.cfm/destiny-as-a-one-stop-shop-part-2.

Ash, K. 2012. "Common Core Drives Interest in Open Education Resources: Spurred by the Adoption of Common-Core Standards by Nearly Every State, the Movement for Open Digital Resources Is Growing as Educators Realign Curricula." *Digital Directions* 6 (1): 42. http://www.edweek.org/dd/articles/2012/10/17/01open.h06.html?tkn=NTOFMxrZ1BSvAwIeHWdbG7nRcERE8nd99JI3&print=1.

Asif, A. 2013. "States Are Slow to Adopt Controversial New Science Standards." Accessed August 12, 2014. http://hechingered.org/content/states-are-slow-to-adopt-controversial-new-science-standards_6355/.

Barbour, M. K., R. Brown, L. H. Waters, R. Hoey, J. L. Hunt, K. Kennedy, C. Ounsworth, A. Powell, and T. Trimm. 2011. "Online and Blended Learning: A Survey of Policy and Practice of K–12 Schools Around the World." Accessed June 5, 2014. http://www.inacol.org/wp-content/uploads/2012/11/iNACOL_IntnlReport2011.pdf.

Bauerlein, M., and S. Stotsky. 2012. Accessed August 12, 2014. "How Common Core's ELA Standards Place College Readiness at Risk." http://pioneer institute.org/?wpdmdl=282&.

Bell, P. 2004. "The Educational Opportunities of Contemporary Controversies in Science." In *Internet Environments for Science Education,* edited by M. C. Linn, E. A. Davis, and P. Bell, pp. 233–260. Mahwah, NJ: Lawrence Erlbaum Associates.

Bethard, S., P. Wetzler, K. Butcher, J. H. Martin, and T. Sumner. 2009. "Automatically Characterizing Resource Quality for Educational Digital Libraries." Paper presented at the Joint Conference on Digital Libraries (JCDL) '09, Austin, Texas, June 15–19, 2009.

Bishop, K. 2013. *The Collection Program in Schools: Concepts and Practices.* Santa Barbara, CA: Libraries Unlimited.

Blank, R. K., and C. Toye. 2007. "50-State Analysis of the Prepartion of Teachers and the Conditions for Teaching: Results from the NCES Schools and Staffing Survey." Accessed May 30, 2014. http://www.ccsso.org/Documents/2007 /50_State_Analysis_of_the_Preparation_2007.pdf.

Boster, F. J., G. S. Meyer, A. J. Roberto, L. Lindsey, R. Smith, C. Inge, and R. E. Strom. 2007. "The Impact of Video Streaming on Mathematics Performance." *Communication Education* 56 (2): 134.

Boston Consulting Group. 2013. "The Open Education Resources Ecosystem: An Evaluation of the OER Movement's Current State and Its Progress Toward Mainstream Adoption." Accessed June 5, 2014. http://www.hewlett.org/sites/default/files/The Open Educational Resources Ecosystem.pdf.

Boyle, A. 1997. "Sputnik Started Space Race, Anxiety: 40 Years Later, Cold War Rivals Cooperate in Space Ventures." Accessed May 1, 2014. http://www.nbcnews.com/id/3077890/ - .U42efS8peAE.

Bransford, J., A. L. Brown, and R. R. Cocking, eds. 2000. *How People Learn: Brain, Mind, Experience, and School.* Washington, DC: National Academy Press.

Campbell, L. M., and P. Barker. 2013. "Activity Data and Paradata: A Briefing Paper." Accessed February 5, 2014. http://publications.cetis.ac.uk/wp-content/uploads/2013 /05/paradataBriefing.pdf.

Carmichael, S. B., G. Martino, K. Porter-Magee, and W. S. Wilson, eds. 2010. *The State of State Standards—and the Common Core—in 2010*. Washington, DC: Thomas B. Fordham Institute.

Collins, S., and P. Levy. 2013. "Guide to the Use of Open Educational Resources in K–12 and Postsecondary Education." Washington, DC: Software & Information Industry Association (SIIA). Accessed August 12, 2014. http://www.siia.net/index.php?option=com_docman&task=doc_download&gid=4029&Itemid=318.

Committee on STEM Education, National Science and Technology Council. 2013. "Federal Science, Technology, Engineering, and Mathematics (STEM) Education 5-Year Strategic Plan." Accessed August 12, 2014. http://www.whitehouse.gov/sites/default /files/microsites/ostp/stem_stratplan_2013.pdf.

Common Core State Standards Initiative [CCSS]. [n.d.-a]. "Common Core State Standards for Mathematics." Accessed June 1, 2014. http://www.corestandards.org/wp-content/uploads/Math_Standards.pdf.

Common Core State Standards Initiative [CCSS]. [n.d.-b]. "Key Shifts in English Language Arts." Accessed August 12, 2014. http://www.corestandards.org/other-resources/key-shifts-in-english-language-arts/.

Common Core State Standards Initiative [CCSS]. (n.d.-c). "Key Shifts in Mathematics." Accessed August 12, 2014. http://www.corestandards.org/other-resources/key-shifts-in-mathematics/.

Common Core State Standards Initiative [CCSS]. 2010. "Common Core State Standards for English Language Arts & Literacy in History/Social Studies, Science, and Technical Subjects." Accessed June 1, 2014. http://www.corestandards.org/wp-content/uploads/ELA_Standards.pdf.

Digital Textbook Collaborative. 2012. "The Digital Textbook Playbook." Accessed August 12, 2014. http://transition.fcc.gov/files/Digital_Textbook_Playbook.pdf.

Drake, E. 2007. "The Teaching and Partnering Responsibilities of Michigan School Library Media Specialists." *Media Spectrum* 33 (3): 46–54.

Duschl, R. A., H. A. Schweingruber, and A. W. Shouse, eds. 2007. *Taking Science to School: Learning and Teaching Science in Grades K–8*. Washington, DC: The National Academies Press.

Ellis, J. D. 2003. "The Influence of the National Science Education Standards on the Science Curriculum." In *What Is the Influence of the National Science Education Standards? Reviewing the Evidence, a Workshop Summary,* edited by K. S. Hollweg and D. Hill, 39–63. Washington, DC: National Academies Press.

Evans, G. E., and M. Zarnosky Saponaro. 2012. *Collection Management Basics*. Santa Barbara, CA: ABC-CLIO.

Everhart, N., M. A. Mardis, and M. Johnston. 2011. "National Board Certified School Librarians' Leadership In Technology Integration: Results of a National Survey." *School Library Media Research* 14. Accessed August 12, 2014. http://www.ala.org/aasl/sites/ala.org.aasl /files/content/aasl-pubsandjournals/slr/vol14 /SLR_NationalBoardCertified_V14.pdf.

Fang, Z. 2014. "Disciplinary Literacy in Science: Developing Science Literacy Through Trade Books." *Journal of Adolescent & Adult Literacy* 57 (4): 274–278.

Finn, C. E., and M. J. Petrilli. 2000. *The State of the Standards 2000.* Washington, DC: Thomas B. Fordham Foundation.

Finn, C. E., M. J. Petrilli, and L. Julian. 2006. *The State of the Standards 2006.* Washington, DC: Thomas B. Fordham Foundation.

Francis, B. H., K. C. Lance, and Z. Lietzau. 2010. "School Librarians Continue to Help Students Achieve Standards: The Third Colorado Study." Accessed May 29, 2014. http://www.lrs.org /documents/closer_look/ CO3_2010_Closer_Look_Report.pdf.

Ginger, K. 2012. "Granularity." Accessed August 12, 2014. http://www.dlese .org/Metadata /collections/granularity.php.

Griffin, A. 2013. "Subjective and Objective Reviews of Instructional Materials." Accessed April 1, 2014. http://simra.us/wp/news/ subjective-and-objective-reviews-of-instructional-materials-2/.

Gross, P., D. Buttrey, U. Goodenough, N. Koertge, L. S. Lerner, M. Schwartz, and R. Schwartz. 2013. "Final Evaluation of the Next Generation Science Standards." Accessed May 10, 2014. http://edex.s3-us-west-2.ama-zonaws.com/publication/pdfs/20130612-NGSS-Final-Review_7.pdf.

Hanson, K., and B. Carlson. 2005. *Effective Access: Teachers' Use of Digital Resources in STEM Teaching.* Newton, MA: Education Development Center, Inc.

Harris, C. 2006. "School Library 2.0: Say Good-Bye to Your Mother's School Library." *School Library Journal* 25 (5): 50.

Hewlett Foundation. 2013. "White Paper: Open Education Resources: Breaking the Lockbox on Education." Accessed August 12, 2014. http://www.hewlett.org/sites/default/files/OER White Paper Nov 22 2013 Final_0.pdf.

Hewlett Foundation. 2014. "Open Educational Resources." Accessed May 5, 2014. http://www.hewlett.org/programs/education/ open-educational-resources.

Hirsch, E. D. 2006. "Building Knowledge: The Case for Bringing Content into the Language Arts Block and for a Knowledge-Rich Curriculum Core for All Children." *American Educator* 30 (1): 8–17.

Hoffman, E. S., and M. A. Mardis. 2008. "Leadership, Collaboration, and Support: Results from a Survey of Science and Mathematics in U.S. Middle

School Media Centers." *Michigan Science Teachers' Association Journal* 53 (2): 29–34.

Holy Bible, King James Version. 1995. Cambridge University Press.

Horizon Research Inc. 2002. "The Influence of the National Science Education Standards on Teachers and Teaching Practice." In *What Is the Influence of the National Science Education Standards? Reviewing the Evidence, a Workshop Summary,* edited by K. S. Hollweg and D. Hill, 91–107. Washington, DC: National Academies Press.

Humphrey, D. C., and R. Carver. 1998. "A Case Study of New York's SSI (NYSSI), 1993–1997." In *SSI Case Studies, Cohort 3: Arkansas and New York,* edited by A. A. Zucker and P. M. Shields. Menlo Park, CA: SRI International.

Itō, M. 2010. *Hanging Out, Messing Around, and Geeking Out : Kids Living and Learning with New Media.* Cambridge, MA: MIT Press.

Jackson, N. M. 2013. "MOOCs Go to K12: Higher Ed Trend Expands to High Schools." *District Administration.* Accessed August 12, 2014. http://www.districtadministration.com/article/moocs-go-k12-higher-ed-trend-expands-high-schools.

Jobrack, B. 2012. "Solving the Textbook-Common Core Conundrum." *Education Week* 31 (37): 31, 36. Accessed August 12, 2014. http://www.edweek.org/ew/articles/2012/08/08 /37jobrack_ep.h31.html?tkn=WXRF2N9OKd0Fpb%2Bd%2FK0gxFrFO%2FnR8Qij9Mln&cmp–ENL-EU-NEWS2.

Kay, R. H. 2012. "Examining Factors That Influence the Effectiveness of Learning Objects in Mathematics Classrooms." *Canadian Journal of Science, Mathematics, and Technology Education* 12 (4): 350–366.

Kay, R. H., and L. Knaack. 2007. "Evaluating the Use of Learning Objects for Secondary School Science." *Journal of Computers in Mathematics and Science Teaching* 26 (4): 261–289. doi: 10.1016/j.compedu.2006.05 .006.

Kay, R. H., and L. Knaack. 2009a. "Analyzing the Effectiveness of Learning Objects for Secondary School Science Classrooms." *Journal of Educational Multimedia and Hypermedia* 18 (2): 113–135.

Kay, R. H., and L. Knaack. 2009b. "Understanding Factors That Influence the Effectiveness of Learning Objects in Secondary School Classrooms." In *Handbook of Research on New Media Literacy at the K-12 Level: Issues and Challenges,* edited by L. T. W. Hin and R. Subramaniam, 419–435. Hershey, PA: Information Science Reference.

Khoo, M., M. Recker, and M. Marlino. 2003. "Understanding Educator Perceptions of 'Quality' in Digital Libraries." Paper presented at the 3rd

ACM/IEEE-CS Joint Conference on Digital Libraries Houston (JCDL), Houston, Texas, May 27–31, 2003.

Kirschenbaum, V. R. 2006. "The Old Way of Reading and the New." *Educational Leadership* 63 (8): 47–50.

Kuhlthau, C. C. 1997. "Learning in Digital Libraries: An Information Search Process Approach." *Library Trends* 45 (4): 708–724.

Kuhlthau, C. C. 2004. *Seeking Meaning: A Process Approach to Library and Information Services*. Westport, CT: Libraries Unlimited.

Lamb, A., and D. Callison. 2005. "Online Learning and Virtual Schools." *School Library Monthly* 21: 29–31.

Lanahan, L. 2002. *Beyond School-Level Internet Access: Support for Instructional Use of Technology*. Washington, DC: National Center for Education Statistics.

Lance, K. C., and D. V. Loertscher. 2001. *Powering Achievement: School Library Programs Make a Difference: The Evidence*. San Jose, CA: Hi Willow Research & Publishing.

Lance, K. C., M. J. Rodney, and C. Hamilton-Pennell. 2000. "How School Librarians Help Kids Achieve Standards: The Second Colorado Study." Accessed August 12, 2014. http://www.lrs.org/documents/lmcstudies/CO/execsumm.pdf.

Lange, B., N. Magee, and S. Montgomery. 2003. "Does Collaboration Boost Student Learning?" *School Library Journal* 49 (6).

Lee, O. 2005. "Science Education with English Language Learners: Synthesis and Research Agenda." *Review of Educational Research* 75 (4): 491–521.

Lemke, J. 2000. "Multimedia Literacy Demands of the Science Curriculum." *Linguistics and Education* 10 (3): 247–271.

Manderson, D. 2012. "Evolving Personalized Learning: Maximizing K12 Expenditures to Support Instructional Reform." Accessed May 10, 2014. http://www.imsglobal.org/i3lc/201211-EvolvingK12PersonalizedLearning-FNL.pdf.

Manduca, C. A., F. P. McMartin, and D. W. Mogk. 2001. "Pathways to Progress: Visions and Plans for Developing NSDL." Accessed June 18, 2005. http://nsdl.comm.nsdl.org/meeting/archives/ smete/meetings/grantees 0901/whitepaper.pdf.

Mardis, M. A. 2003. "If We Build It, Will They Come? An Overview of the Issues in K–12 Digital Libraries." In *Developing Digital Libraries for K–12 Education*, edited by M. Mardis. Syracuse, NY: ERIC Information Technology Clearinghouse.

Mardis, M. A. 2004. "Infusing Science into Middle School Media Centers: Obstacles and Strategies. A Final Report for the Institute for Library

& Information Literacy Education (ILILE) National Research Grant Program."

Mardis, M. A. 2005. "The Relationship Between School Library Media Programs and Science Achievement in Michigan Middle Schools." Ed.D. doctoral diss., Eastern Michigan University, Ypsilanti.

Mardis, M. A. 2006a. "Science Teacher and School Library Media Specialist Roles: Mutually Reinforcing Perspectives As Defined by National Guidelines." In *Educational Media and Technology Yearbook,* edited by M. Orey, V. McClendon, and R. M. Branch, vol. 31, 169–178. Westport, CT: Libraries Unlimited.

Mardis, M. A. 2006b. "Science-Related Topics in School Library Media Periodicals: An Analysis of Electronic Citation Content from 1998–2004." *School Libraries Worldwide* 12 (2): 1–15.

Mardis, M. A. 2007. "School Libraries and Science Achievement: A View from Michigan's Middle Schools." *School Library Media Research* 10.

Mardis, M. A. 2008. "Children's Questions About Science: Preliminary Results of an Analysis of Digital Library Reference Questions." Paper presented at the People Transforming Information—Information Transforming People: Proceedings of the Annual Meeting of American Society for Information Science and Technology (ASIST), Columbus, Ohio, October 24–29, 2008.

Mardis, M. A. 2009. "Viewing Michigan's Digital Future: Results of a Survey of Educators' Use of Digital Video in the United States." *Learning, Media & Technology* 34 (3): 243–257. doi: 10.1080/17439880903141539.

Mardis, M. A. 2011. "Reflections on School Library as Place, School Library as Space." *School Libraries Worldwide* 17 (1): i–iv.

Mardis, M. A., T. ElBasri, S. K. Norton, and J. Newsum. 2012. "The New Digital Lives of U.S. Teachers: A Research Synthesis and Trends to Watch." *School Libraries Worldwide* 18 (1): 70–86.

Mardis, M. A., and N. Everhart. 2013. "From Paper to Pixel: Digital Textbooks and Florida Schools." In *Educational Media and Technology Yearbook,* edited by M. Orey, S. A. Jones, and R. M. Branch, vol. 37, pp. 93–118. New York, NY: Springer.

Mardis, M. A., and E. S. Hoffman. 2007a. "Collection and Collaboration: Science in Michigan Middle School Media Centers." *School Library Media Research*, 10. Accessed August 13, 2014. http://www.ala.org/aasl/aaslpubsandjournals/slmrb/slmrcontents/volume10/mardis_collection andcollaboration.

Mardis, M. A., and E. S. Hoffman. 2007b. "Collection and Collaboration: Science in Michigan Middle School Media Centers." *Media Spectrum* 33 (3): 44–58.

Mardis, M. A., and K. Howe. 2010. "STEM for Our Students: Content or Co-Conspiracy?" *Knowledge Quest* 39 (2): 8–11.

Mardis, M. A., and L. Zia. 2003. "Leading the Wave of Science and Mathematics Learning Innovation." *Knowledge Quest* 31: 8–9.

McIlvain, E. 2010. "NSDL as a Teacher Empower Point. " *Knowledge Quest* 39 (2): 54–63.

Mickey, K., and K. Meaney. 2010. *Simba Information's 2010 National Textbook Adoption Scorecard and 2011 Outlook.* Stamford, CT: Simba Information.

Mickey, K., and K. Meaney. 2011. *Simba Information's 2011 National Textbook Adoption Scorecard and 2012 Outlook.* Stamford, CT: Simba Information.

Mickey, K., and K. Meaney. 2013. *Getting Ready for the Common Core 2013– 2014.* Stamford, CT: Simba Information, Inc.

National Academy of Education [NAE]. 2009. "Science and Mathematics Education: Education Policy White Paper." Accessed May 25, 2010. http://www.naeducation.org/Science_and_Mathematics_Education_White_Paper.pdf.

National Center for Education Statistics [NCES]. 2007. *The Condition of Education 2007.* Washington, DC: U.S. Department of Education.

National Center for Education Statistics [NCES]. 2013. *The Nation's Report Card: A First Look: 2013 Mathematics and Reading.* Washington, DC: Institute of Education Sciences, U.S. Department of Education.

National Center for Education Statistics [NCES]. 2014. *Local Education Agency (School District) Universe Survey, 2011–12 v.1a; State Nonfiscal Public Elementary/Secondary Education Survey, 2011–12 v.1a.*

National Council of Teachers of Mathematics [NCTM]. 2014. *Principles to Actions: Ensuring Mathematical Success for All.* Reston, VA: NCTM, National Council of Teachers of Mathematics.

National Council on Teacher Quality. 2014. "2013 State Teacher Policy Yearbook." Accessed May 20, 2014. http://www.nctq.org/dmsView /2013 _State_Teacher_Policy_Yearbook_National_Summary_NCTQ_Report.

National Research Council [NRC]. 1996. *National Science Education Standards.* Washington DC: National Academy Press.

National Research Council [NRC]. 2007. *Taking Science to School: Learning and Teaching Science in Grades K–8.* Washington, DC: The National Academies Press.

National Science Board [NSB]. 2006. *Science and Engineering Indicators 2006.* Vol. 2006. Washington, DC: National Science Foundation.

National Science Board [NSB]. 2008. *Science and Engineering Indicators 2008.* Arlington, VA: National Science Foundation.

National Science Board [NSB]. 2010. "Preparing the Next Generation of STEM Innovators: Identifying and Developing Our Nation's Human Capital." Accessed August 13, 2014. http://nsf.gov/nsb/publications/2010/nsb1033.pdf.

National Science Board [NSB]. 2014. *Science and Engineering Indicators 2014*. Arlington, VA: National Science Foundation.

National Science Digital Library [NSDL]. 2012. "Collection and Resource Quality Checklist." Accessed June 1, 2014. http://nsdl.org/content/files/pdfs/resource_quality_chklst.pdf.

National Science Digital Library [NSDL]. 2013. *OER Digital Content: A Combined Voices Meeting, June 27–30, 2013*. University Corporation for Atmospheric Research [UCAR]. Boulder, CO.

National Science Foundation [NSF]. 2007. *Cyberinfrastructure Vision for 21st Century Discovery*. Arlington, VA: National Science Foundation.

National Science Teachers Association [NSTA]. 2011. "NSTA Position Statement: Quality Science Education and 21st-Century Skills." Accessed August 13, 2014. http://www.nsta.org/about/positions/21stcentury.aspx?lid=exp.

Nisonger, T. E. 2000. "Collection Development in an Electronic Environment." *Library Trends* 48 (4): 639–922 (Special Issue).

O'Reilly, T., and D. S. McNamara. 2007. "The Impact of Science Knowledge, Reading Skill, and Reading Strategy Knowledge on More Traditional 'High Stakes' Measures of High School Students' Science Achievement." *American Educational Research Journal* 44 (1): 161–196.

Office of Educational Technology. 2013. *Expanding Evidence Approaches for Learning in a Digital World*. Washington, DC: U.S. Department of Education.

Okerson, A. 2000. "Are We There Yet? Online E-Resources Ten Years After." *Library Trends* 48 (4), 671–693.

Organisation for Economic Cooperation and Development [OECD]. 2010. *PISA 2009 Results: What Students Know and Can Do—Student Performance in Reading, Mathematics and Science* (Volume I). http://dx.doi.org/10.1787/9789264091450-en.

Organisation for Economic Cooperation and Development [OECD]. 2014. *PISA 2012 Results: What Students Know and Can Do—Student Performance in Mathematics, Reading and Science* (Volume I, revised edition). http://dx.doi.org/10.1787/9789264201118-en.

Pattee, A. 2014. *Developing Library Collections for Today's Young Adults*. Lanham, MD: Scarecrow Press, Inc.

Perrault, A. M. 2007. "An Exploratory Study of Biology Teacher's Online Information Seeking Practices." *School Library Research* 10. Accessed

September 8, 2014 http://www.ala.org/ala /slr/vol10/SLMR_ExploratoryStudy_Vol10.pdf.

Pitschmann, L. A. 2001. "Building Sustainable Collections of Free Third-Party Web Resources." Accessed June 1, 2014. http://www.clir.org/pubs/ reports/reports/pub98/pub98.pdf.

Porcello, D., and S. Hsi. 2013. "Curating and Crowdsourcing Online Education Resources." *Science* 34 (6143): 240–241. doi: 10.1126/ science.1234722.

Price, L. 2007. "Lecturers' vs. Students' Perceptions of the Accessibility of Instructional Materials." *Instructional Science* 35 (4): 317–341. doi: 10.1007/s11251-006-9009-y.

Project Tomorrow. 2010. "Unleashing the Future: Educators 'Speak Up' About the Use of Emerging Technologies for Learning; Speak Up 2009 National Findings from Teachers, Aspiring Teachers, and Administrators." Accessed August 13, 2014. http://www.tomorrow.org/speakup/ pdfs/SU09UnleashingTheFuture.pdf.

Project Tomorrow. 2012a. "Mapping a Personalized Learning Journey—K–12 Students and Parents Connect the Dots with Digital Learning." Accessed August 13, 2014. http://www.tomorrow.org/speakup/pdfs/ SU11_PersonalizedLearning_Students.pdf.

Project Tomorrow. 2012b. "Personalizing the Classroom Experience—Teachers, Librarians and Administrators Connect the Dots with Digital Learning." August 13, 2014. http://www.tomorrow.org/speakup/SU11_Personal izedClassroom_EducatorsReport.html.

Project Tomorrow. 2014. "The Digtal Learning Playbook: Advancing College and Career Ready Skill Development in K–12 Schools. Speak Up 2013 Findings from Educators and Parents." Accessed August 13, 2014. http://www.tomorrow.org/speakup/SU13_EducatorsReportTEXT.html.

Project Tomorrow, and PASCO Scientific. 2008. "Inspiring the Next Generation of Innovators: Students, Parents, and Educators Speak Up About Science Education." Accesed August 13, 2014. http://www .tomorrow.org/speakup/pdfs/Inspiring_the_next_generation_of _innovators.pdf.

Quinn, H., H. Schweingruber, and T. Keller. 2012. *A Framework for K–12 Science Education: Practices, Crosscutting Concepts, and Core Ideas.* Washington, DC: The National Academies Press.

Recker, M., H. Leary, A. Walker, A. Diekema, P. Wetzler, T. Sumner, and J. H. Martin. 2011. "Modeling Teacher Ratings of Online Resources: A Human Machine Approach to Quality." Paper presented at the American Educational Research Association (AERA) Annual Meeting, New Orleans, Louisiana, April 8–11.

Recker, M., A. Walker, S. Giersch, X. Mao, S. Halioris, B. Palmer, D. Johnson, H. Leary, and M. B. Robertshaw. 2007. "A Study of Teachers' Use of Online Learning Resources to Design Classroom Activities." *New Review of Hypermedia and Multimethods* 13 (2), 117–134. doi: 10.1080/13614560701709846.

Roschelle, J. 1995. "Learning in Interactive Environments: Prior Knowledge and New Experience." In *Public Institutions for Personal Learning: Establishing a Research Agenda*, edited by J. H. Falk and L. D. Dierking. Washington, DC: American Association of Museums.

Roseman, J. E., L. Stern, and M. Koppal. 2010. "A Method for Analyzing the Coherence of High School Biology Textbooks." *Journal of Research in Science Teaching* 47 (1): 47–70. doi: 10.1002/tea.20305.

Rosenbaum, S. 2011. *Curation Nation: Why the Future of Content Is Context.* New York, NY: McGraw Hill.

Samuels, A. C. 2012. "Big Districts Push for Teaching Texts Aligned to Common Core." *Education Week* 36 (10).

Scholastic. 2008. *School Libraries Work! Third ed.* Accessed August 13, 2014. http://www2.scholastic.com/content/collateral_resources/pdf/s/slw3_2008.pdf.

School Library Journal. 2013. "School Technology Survey: U.S. School Libraries 2013." http://www.slj.com/downloads/slj-technology-survey/.

Schultz-Jones, B., and C. Ledbetter. 2009. "Building Relationships in the School Social Network: Science Teachers and School Library Media Specialists Report Key Dimensions." *School Libraries Worldwide* 15 (2): 23–48.

Schwan, S., and R. Riempp. 2004. "The Cognitive Benefits of Interactive Videos: Learning to Tie Nautical Knots." *Learning and Instruction* 14 (3): 293–305.

SETDA and Education Counsel LLC. 2014. "The Accessibility of Learning Content for All Students, Including Students with Disabilities, Must Be Addressed In the Shift to Digital Instructional Materials." Accessed June 1, 2014. http://www.setda.org/wp-content/uploads/2014/03/SETDA_PolicyBrief_Accessibility_FNL.5.29.pdf.

Shank, J. D. 2014. *Interactive Open Educational Resources: A Guide to Finding, Choosing, and Using What's Out There to Transform College Teaching.* San Francisco, CA: Jossey-Bass.

Shapiro, A. R. 2012. "Between Training and Popularization: Regulating Science Textbooks in Secondary Education." *Isis* 103 (1): 99–110. doi: 10.1086/664981.

Simba Information. 2014. *2013 National Instructional Materials Adoption Scorecard and 2014 Forecast.* Stamford, CT: Simba Information.

Slygh, G. L. 2000. "Shake, Rattle, and Role! The Effects of Professional Community on the Collaborative Role of the School Librarian." PhD diss., University of Wisconsin–Madison.

Spiegel, D. L. 1989. "Instructional Resources: Evaluating Instructional Materials." *The Reading Teacher* 43 (1): 72–73. doi: 10.2307/20140207.

Stern, L., and J. E. Roseman. 2004. "Can Middle-School Science Textbooks Help Students Learn Important Ideas? Findings from Project 2061's Curriculum Evaluation Study: Life Science." *Journal of Research in Science Teaching* 41 (6): 538–568. doi: 10.1002/tea.20019.

Straessle, G. A. 2000. *Teachers' and Administrators' Perceptions and Expectations of the Instructional Consultation Role of the Library Media Specialist.* Unpublished PhD diss., Pacific Lutheran University, Parkland, WA.

Strauss, V. 2014. "Everything You Need to Know about Common Core—Ravitch." *Washington Post.* Accesed August 13, 2014. http://www.washingtonpost.com/blogs/answer-sheet/wp/2014/01/18/everything-you-need-to-know-about-common-core-ravitch/

Subramaniam, M., J. Ahn, A. Waugh, N. Greene Taylor, A. Druin, K. R. Fleischmann, and G. Walsh. 2013. "Crosswalk Between the Framework for K–12 Science Education and Standards for the 21st-Century Learner: School Librarians as the Crucial Link." *School Library Research* 16. Accessed August 13, 2014. http://www.ala.org/aasl/sites/ala.org.aasl/files/content /aaslpubsandjournals/slr/vol16/SLR_Crosswalkbetween FrameworkStandards_V16.pdf/

Trygstad, P. J., P. S. Smith, E. R. Banilower, and M. M. Nelson. 2013. "The Status of Elementary Science Education: Are We Ready for the Next Generation Science Standards?" Accessed June 1, 2014. http://www.horizon-research.com/horizonresearchwp/wp-content/uploads/2013/12/The-Status-of-Elementary-Science-Education_paper.pdf.

Ulerick, S. L. [n.d.]. "Using Textbooks for Meaningful Learning in Science." Accessed July 12, 2004. http://www.educ.sfu.ca/narsite/publications/research/textbook2.htm.

United States Department of Education. 2014. "Race to the Top Fund." Accessed August 13, 2014. http://www2.ed.gov/programs/racetothetop/index.html.

United States National Commission on Excellence in Education and United States Department of Education. 1983. *A Nation at Risk: The Imperative for Educational Reform.* Washington, DC: National Commission on Excellence in Education.

Valenza, J. 2007. "NeverEnding Search" (blog). Accessed December 13, 2007. http://www.schoollibraryjournal.com/blog/1340000334.html.

Watson, J. S. 2003. "Examining Perceptions of the Science Fair Project: Content or Process?" *School Library Media Research* 6.

Weiss, I. R., E. R. Banilower, K. C. McMahon, and P. S. Smith. 2001. *Report of the 2000 National Survey of Science and Mathematics Education.* Chapel Hill, NC: Horizon Research.

Wetzler, P., S. Bethard, H. Leary, K., Butcher, S. D. Bahreni, J. Zhao, J. Martin, and T. Sumner. 2013. "Characterizing and Predicting the Multifaceted Nature of Quality in Educational Web Resources." *ACM Transactions on Interactive Intelligent Systems* 3 (3): 15:11–15:25. doi: 10.1145/2533670.2533673.

Wiley, D. A. 2000. "Connecting Learning Objects to Instructional Design Theory: A Definition, a Metaphor, and a Taxonomy." In *The Instructional Use of Learning Objects: Online Version,* edited by D. A. Wiley. 1–35. AccessedAugust 13, 2014. http://reusability.org/read/chapters/wiley.doc.

Windschitl, M., and J. Thompson. 2006. "Transcending Simple Forms of School Science Investigation: The Impact of Preservice Instruction on Teachers' Understandings of Model-Based Inquiry." *American Educational Research Journal* 43(4): 783–836.

Yaron, D. 2009. "Reflections on the NSDL." Accessed May 10, 2014. http://nsdlreflections.wordpress.com/2009/01/12/reflections-on-the-nsdl-by-david-yaron/ - more-227.

Yerrick, R., D. L. Ross, and P. E. Molebash. 2003–2004. "Promoting Equity with Digital Video." *Learning and Leading with Technology* 31 (4): 16–19.

Young, T. E. 2001. "Library 'Science' Rules." *The Book Report* 19 (5): 25–27.

Zia, L. L. 2005. "The NSF National Science, Technology, Engineering and Mathematics Education Digital Library Program: New Project from Fiscal Year 2004." *D-Lib Magazine.* Accesssed August 13, 2014. http://www.dlib.org/dlib/march05/zia/03zia.html.

Index

About the Author

MARCIA A. MARDIS, EdD, is an associate professor at Florida State University's School of Information in Tallahassee, Florida. A former school administrator and school librarian, Mardis has authored numerous scholarly publications and leads many state, federal, and international STEM-focused school library projects. Mardis researches and writes about the intersection of school libraries, digital libraries, and K–12 STEM education.